CHILDREN'S MISCELLANY
VOLUME THREE

Even more useless information
that's essential to know

CHILDREN'S MISCELLANY
VOLUME THREE
VOLUME THREE

Buster
Books

First published in Great Britain in 2006 by Buster Books,
an imprint of Michael O'Mara Books Limited
9 Lion Yard
Tremadoc Road
London SW4 7NQ

A CIP catalogue record for this book is available from the British Library.

ISBN-10: 1-905158-42-4
ISBN-13: 978-1-905158-42-3

10 9 8 7 6 5 4 3 2 1

www.mombooks.com/busterbooks

Printed and bound in China by Leo Paper Products

Written by Guy Macdonald
Edited by Ellen Bailey
Contributions by Kate Byrne, Ariane Durkin and Elizabeth Scoggins
Interior illustrations by Niki Catlow
Cover illustration by Jane Massey

CONTENTS

CONTENTS

CONTENTS

CONTENTS

CONTENTS

——THINGS THAT THERE SHOULD BE WORDS—— FOR THAT THERE AREN'T

The strangely pleasant feeling of desperately needing the toilet

The feeling of disappointment you get when you receive the same present twice

An itch that you can only get rid of by scratching another part of your body

The shock of hearing your own name spoken during a daydream in class

The extra-delicious taste that food has when you can only have one mouthful

The far-away feeling you get in your head when you read something out loud in front of lots of people

The love you feel for someone (usually a brother or sister) that can only be expressed by annoying them

The shame of being told off by a friend's parent

> Outer space begins 100km (62 miles) above the Earth's surface. The line where outer space begins is called the Kármán line.

————————A BILLION AGO————————

A billion seconds ago, your parents were children.

A billion minutes ago, the Roman Empire was booming.

A billion hours ago, Neanderthals lived in Europe and Asia.

A billion months ago, dinosaurs ruled the Earth.

A billion years ago, primitive life evolved.

──── THE DIFFERENCE BETWEEN TANGERINES, ──── SATSUMAS, CLEMENTINES AND ORANGES

ORANGE
Thought to be a cross between a pomelo (a pale-green fruit bigger than a grapefruit) and a tangerine. (A grapefruit is a cross between a pomelo and an orange.)

MANDARIN ORANGE
Resembles an orange, but is shaped like a flattened sphere. It comes in several varieties including the tangerine, satsuma and clementine.

SATSUMA
Sweet, seedless and smaller than an orange. The skin can be peeled easily. First exported from Satsuma Province in Japan, where satsumas are called *mikan*.

TANGOR
A cross between a mandarin and an orange. Thin, easy-to-peel rind and pale-orange pulp that tastes spicy and tart.

CLEMENTINE
Smooth, glossy, vibrant orange skin that is thin and easy to peel. They separate easily into 8 to 12 juicy, sweet-tasting segments.

TANGERINE
Has dimpled skin that peels off easily. Smaller than an orange, but heavy for its size. The name comes from Tangier, a port in Morocco from which the first tangerines were shipped to Europe.

──── THE LAYERS OF EARTH'S ATMOSPHERE ────

Troposphere.....................................0—14.5km (0—9 miles) above Earth

Stratosphere..............................14.5—50km (9—31 miles) above Earth

Mesosphere................................50—85km (31—53 miles) above Earth

Thermosphere.....................85—600km (53—372 miles) above Earth

Exosphere..600km+ (372 miles+) above Earth

SMELLY CHEESES

Vieux Boulogne
Pont l'Évêque
Munster
Camembert
Gammelost
Limburger
Brie de Meaux
Roquefort
Reblochon
Livarot
Banon
Gorgonzola
Époisses de Bourgogne
Stinking Bishop

REAL SONIC WEAPONS

Sonic weapons are weapons that use sound
waves to deter or injure the enemy.

INFRASONIC SIREN
Modern cruise ships
have experimented with
infrasonic sirens to repel the
enemy at sea. The low-
frequency sound can make
concrete walls crumble
and humans violently ill.

ANTI-FROGMAN WEAPON
A ship can sound its
ordinary navigation sonar to
deter enemy scuba divers.
The sound waves make
divers disorientated and they
either panic and drown, or
are forced to the surface.

SONIC BULLETS
These high-power beams
of ultrasound can measure
up to 145 decibels loud. The
sound waves stop people
in their tracks.

INFRASONIC GUN
In the 1950s the first
infrasonic gun was
immediately classified as
'almost lethal' when it
made the internal organs
of the test subjects bleed.
The gun made the
laboratory shake violently,
even on low power.

THINGS NOT TO TREAD ON WHEN
PADDLING IN THE SEA

Portuguese man-of-war.......................Jellyfish with stinging tentacles

Stinging seaweed....................Venomous animal disguised as a plant

Fire coral.............................Looks like coral but has stinging tentacles

Stonefish.........................Looks like a stone but has poisonous spines

Sea urchin............Has poisonous spines that break off in your foot

Stingray...Fish with a razor-sharp spine and
stinging tail that lies in the sand

Blue-ringed octopus...............The size of a tennis ball, with poison
powerful enough to kill a human in minutes

INEXPENSIVE COLLECTIBLES

Chewing-gum packets • Aeroplane sick bags
Crisp packets • Rubber ducks • Matchboxes
Train tickets • Four-leaf clovers • Fruit stickers
Human teeth • Buttons • Ballpoint pens
Fridge magnets • Fizzy-drink cans

PHASES OF THE MOON

On average, the Moon takes 29½ days to complete one orbit around the Earth. This is known as a lunar month. During this time, the Moon goes through a complete cycle from new Moon to full Moon and back again. The phases are:

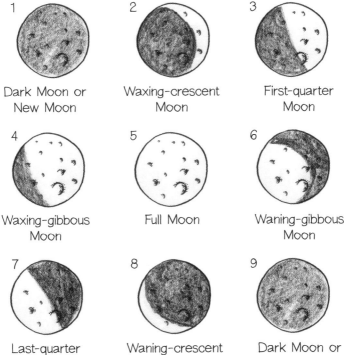

1 — Dark Moon or New Moon

2 — Waxing-crescent Moon

3 — First-quarter Moon

4 — Waxing-gibbous Moon

5 — Full Moon

6 — Waning-gibbous Moon

7 — Last-quarter Moon

8 — Waning-crescent Moon

9 — Dark Moon or New Moon

In the southern hemisphere, the above is reversed so that a waxing-crescent Moon is seen as the left side of the Moon, and a waning-crescent Moon is seen as the right side of the Moon.

> Paraguay is the only country in the world whose national flag has two different sides.

───POISONOUS PLANTS───

Deadly nightshade • Hemlock
Holly • Death cap mushroom
Mistletoe • Iris • Yew

───HOW TO KEEP A DIARY───

1. Make sure that your diary is special to you. You might want to cover a blank pad with paper, fabric or photos.

2. Don't feel that you have to write something every day.

3. Focus on the details of your day: who you saw, what you did, where you went and how you felt.

5. Don't whinge in it. Write boldly.

4. If you are writing sensational material about people you know, disguise their identities with code names.

6. It may help to address your entries to an imaginary person.

7. Keep it somewhere safe and away from prying eyes.

8. Just to be extra sure that no one will ever read it, write *MY BOOK OF ALGEBRA* on the cover.

───FAST FLIERS───

Peregrine falcon...270kph (168mph)

Spine-tailed swift..171kph (106mph)

Frigate bird..153kph (95mph)

Spur-winged goose...142kph (88mph)

Red-breasted merganser......................................129kph (80mph)

─────────REAL-LIFE SUPERHEROES─────────

STRETCHY MAN

British man Gary Turner can stretch his skin to a length of 15.8cm (6.2in). By pulling the skin of his neck up and the skin of his forehead down, he can completely cover his whole face. On 27 November 2004, he clipped 159 wooden clothes pegs to his face, earning himself a world record.

MR EAT EVERYTHING

In 1959 Michel Lotito of France developed a taste for metal and glass. So far he has eaten 18 bicycles, 15 supermarket trolleys, 7 TV sets, 2 beds, 1 pair of skis and 1 Cessna light aircraft.

THE HUMAN LIGHTNING CONDUCTOR

Roy C. Sullivan of the USA has been struck by lightning no fewer than seven times. He has survived each strike, but suffered the following injuries:

1942 – lost a big toenail

1969 – lost both eyebrows

1970 – left shoulder burned

1972 – hair caught fire

1973 – legs burned, hair singed

1976 – ankle hurt

1977 – stomach and chest burned

──COUNTRIES WHOSE NAMES BEGIN AND END── WITH THE SAME LETTER

Albania	Australia
Algeria	Austria
Andorra	Czech Republic
Angola	St Kitts and Nevis
Antigua and Barbuda	St Vincent and the Grenadines
Argentina	Seychelles
Armenia	Solomon Islands

THE THREE-CARD-MONTE SCAM

1. The scammer shows three playing cards to the audience. One of the cards is a queen.

2. The three cards are placed face-down on a table.

3. The scammer moves the cards around, changing their positions, then invites the audience to place bets on which one is the queen.

4. If the audience are sceptical and hang back, an accomplice places a bet and wins.

5. Encouraged by this, the audience start placing bets.

6. The scammer secretly swaps the queen for a different card to ensure that the members of the audience always lose.

7. To keep the bets coming in, every so often the scammer secretly reintroduces the queen and lets someone win. If he is a successful con artist, no one will even realize they are being conned.

BIRD CALLS

Tawny owl	'Hoo hoo-hooo hoo-o-o'
Peregrine falcon	'Haak-haak-haak kee-keeee-eeee wheee-ip'
Wren	'Chit chiti tzerr'
Blue tit	'Tsee-tsee-tsee-tsisisisisisi'
Nuthatch	'Pew pew pew chwee chwee'
Bittern	'Boom ker-whoomp'
Middle-spotted woodpecker	'Kvek-kvek-kvek kuk-uk kuk-uk'
Brent goose	'Kurr-onk kurr-onk kurr-onk'
Laughing gull	'hah-hah-hah hoo-hoo hah-hah-hah'
Wood pigeon	'Coo-ooo-coo-cu-ooo coo-coo-cu-coo'
Egyptian vulture	'Silent'

TEN RULES OF DUELLING

1. You may use a duel to restore honour if someone has offended you.
2. Challenges are never delivered at night.
3. The duel must take place within a month of the challenge being delivered.
4. The challenged has the right to choose the weapon and the location of the duel.
5. Each combatant nominates a 'second' of equal rank in society. The second acts as a go-between — first attempting reconciliation between the parties, and then, if this fails, fixing the time and terms of the duel.
6. The duellists start at an agreed distance from each other, armed with swords or pistols.
7. Seconds must reattempt reconciliation after the specified time or number of shots or blows.
8. In the case of pistols, a misfire is counted as a shot.
9. If seconds disagree on anything, they may themselves duel. They should position themselves at right-angles to the challengers to form a cross.
10. Any wound that causes the hand to shake ends the duel.

FUN DUELLING WEAPONS

Bananas
Water pistols
Flour bombs
Snowballs
Light sabres
Custard pies
Paper aeroplanes
Back-to-front speaking

BUBBLEGUM

The first bubblegum was developed in 1906. It was named 'Blibber-Blubber'.

In 1928, the bubblegum recipe was improved by an American called Walter Diemer, resulting in the first widely sold bubblegum, 'Dubble Bubble'. Diemer coloured his creation pink because it was the only food colouring he had.

Today over 100,000 tons of bubblegum are chewed every year.

HOW TO BLOW A BUBBLEGUM BUBBLE

1. Put a big piece of bubblegum in your mouth.

2. Chew it until it's thin and stretchy.

3. Use your tongue to flatten the gum across the backs of your top and bottom front teeth.

4. Push the middle of the gum out between your teeth while forming a seal all the way around the gum with your lips.

5. Blow into the stretched gum.

TIPS FOR REMOVING GUM FROM HAIR AND CLOTHING

1. Rub the gum with an ice cube. This will harden the gum, making it easier to pick and scratch off.

2. Squeeze lemon juice on the gum. This will help reduce its stickiness.

3. Put a few drops of cooking oil or peanut butter on a toothbrush and scrub the gum.

> The advertising slogan 'Pepsi gives you life' was mistranslated into Chinese to 'Pepsi brings your ancestors back from the grave.'

PLACES TO HIDE A SECRET MESSAGE

Under a loose floorboard • In the notch of a tree
Under your mattress • On the ledge inside a chimney
Behind a picture frame • In a watertight jar in a pond

CAR JOURNEY GAMES

I SPY
Look around and choose an object for the other passengers
to guess. Let them know the letter the object begins with by
saying 'I spy with my little eye something beginning with...' The
first person to guess correctly takes the next turn.

SCISSORS, PAPER, STONE
Hold your right hand in a fist and get a friend to do the same.
Count to three out loud and then, at the same time, each use
your hand to mime either a pair of scissors (first two fingers
held open), a piece of paper (a flat hand) or a stone (a fist).
Scissors beat (cut) paper. Paper beats (covers) stone. Stone
beats (blunts) scissors.

THE ALPHABET GAME
Choose a category such as 'things that smell bad', 'wild
animals', or 'famous people', and think of an example to fit the
chosen category for each letter of the alphabet.

FIRST TO 20
Each choose something to count: for example, yellow cars,
Belgian lorries or squashed animals. The first to count 20 of
their chosen category wins.

SING THE MILEAGE SONG
Substitute for 'X' the number of miles you have left to drive
in the following song: 'X more miles to go, X more miles
of sorrow, X more miles in this old car and we'll
be there tomorrow.'

APOLOGIZE PROFUSELY FOR SINGING THE MILEAGE SONG
Say sorry over and over until you reach your destination.

EXTREME CHALLENGES

THE POLAR CHALLENGE
592-km (368-mile) trek
to the North Pole.
X-factor: Freezing conditions.

DAKAR MOTOR RALLY
9,000-km (5,600-mile) motor
race across North Africa.
X-factor: The Sahara Desert.

VENDÉE GLOBE
37,000-km (23,000-mile),
non-stop, solo sail
around the world.
X-factor: Storms.

DEATH VALLEY
ULTRA-MARATHON
217-km (135-mile) run across
America's Wild West.
X-factor: Soaring
temperatures.

TEXAS WATER SAFARI
Three-day, 421-km (262-
mile), non-stop canoe race,
along the Colorado River
to the Gulf of Mexico.
X-factor: Swirling currents.

WESTERN STATES
TRAIL RIDE
161-km (100-mile), 24-hour
horse race across the
Sierra Nevada Mountains.
X-factor: Saddle sores.

LA RUTA DE LOS
CONQUISTADORES
483-km (300-mile),
three-day mountain-bike
race in the Costa
Rican jungle.
X-factor: Two volcanoes.

SEAFARING SUPERSTITIONS

GOOD LUCK

Seeing a black cat before
setting sail

Placing a silver coin under
the masthead

Seeing a swallow

Dolphins swimming
alongside the ship

The feather of a wren killed
on New Year's Day

BAD LUCK

Crossing paths with a
redhead before setting sail

Looking back to port once
you have set sail

Setting sail on a Friday

Killing an albatross

Hearing church bells

Saying the word 'drowned'

Drowning

AVIATION LIGHT SIGNALS

If radio communication breaks down, air traffic control uses a light gun to signal messages to the aircraft.

Steady green...Cleared to land

Flashing green..Cleared to approach airport

Steady red......................Continue circling, give way to other aircraft

Flashing red...Airport unsafe, do not land

Alternating red and green..............................Danger, continue current action with caution

---

> The word television comes from the Greek *tele* for 'far' and Latin *visio* for 'sight'.

IS THIS GO-CART MOVING?

Stare at the wheels of the go-cart below. Jiggle the book and see if you can make the wheels turn.

WHO'S WHO IN A FILM CREW

Producer..In charge of raising money

Director..............Responsible for content of film and performances

Scriptwriter..Writes the screenplay

Location manager......................................Finds the right places to film

Grip..In charge of lighting and rigging

Dolly grip................In charge of moving cameras on the dolly track

Gaffer..Head of the electrical department

Visual effects supervisor....................................Creates special effects

Foley artist......................................Creates and records sound effects

Best boy..Technical assistant

Swing gang...........Team that makes last-minute changes to the set

ALMOST SURELY

In probability theory, the phrase 'almost surely' has a precise
meaning. It is an event that has zero probability of *not*
occurring — i.e. it is 'almost surely' going to happen, even
though it is still possible that it might not occur.

——————— ACCIDENTALLY TASTY ———————

CHOCOLATE CHIP COOKIES
In the 1930s, Ruth Wakefield, the owner of the Toll House Inn in Massachusetts, USA, sprinkled chocolate bits into her cookie mixture expecting them to melt. But the chocolate bits held their shape, and instead of making chocolate biscuits, she got butter biscuits full of chocolate chips.

CORNFLAKES
While working in a hospital in the US state of Michigan in 1884, the Kellogg brothers left a pot of wheat-flour mixture to stand too long. Wondering what would happen, they put the stale wheat through the rollers anyway. Instead of the usual long sheet of dough, they got flakes of wheat that they roasted and served to their patients. They were soon selling their tasty invention under the name 'Granose'.

CRÈME BRULÉE
Far from being a traditional French dish, it is said that crème brulée or 'burnt cream' originated in 17th-century England. Having accidentally scorched a bowl of custard sprinkled with sugar, the chef at Trinity College, part of Cambridge University, served up the caramelized offering as a new dish. At the university it is still known as 'Trinity College cream'.

——————— PAGAN FESTIVALS ———————

Yule.....................Marks the shortest day of the year, winter solstice

Imbolc...............Celebrates the lengthening of the days, 2 February

Ostara..Festival of spring, spring equinox

Beltane....................................Celebrates the onset of summer, 1 May

Litha.................Marks the longest day of the year, summer solstice

Lammas...Harvest festival, 1 August

Mabon...Festival of autumn, autumn equinox

Samhain............................The beginning of the dark half of the year,
31 October

----------------- THE RICHTER SCALE -----------------

In 1935, the US seismologist (earthquake expert) Charles Richter developed a scale for measuring the strength of earthquakes, based on the magnitude of vibrations in the ground. Each level on the scale is ten times greater than the preceding one.

0 to 2....................................Detected by instruments, but not humans

3 to 4..Hanging lights sway, windows rattle

5..............At epicentre, objects fall off shelves and windows shatter

6..................Within 10km (6 miles), chimneys crack and roof tiles fall

7..........Within 100km (60 miles), the ground cracks and pipes burst

8..............................Within 300km (185 miles), buildings are destroyed

9.....................................Within 1,000km (620 miles), waves ripple the
ground, and buildings and bridges fall

-----------------VIKING NAMES-----------------

Bjorn Ironside • Eric Bloodaxe
Ivar the Boneless • Orvar-odd
Harold Bluetooth • Sigrid the Haughty
Sigurd Snake-eye • Halfdan the Black
Hrolf the Walker • Ingvar the Far-travelled

To work out your own Viking name, either:

1. Follow your first name with the word 'blood-' and the name of your favourite weapon. For example, if your name is Daniel and your favourite weapon is your super-strong thumb, your Viking name would be Daniel Bloodthumb.

or:

2. Follow your first name with the word 'the' and then your most memorable quality – the more evil the better. For example, if your name is James and you are famous for your deadly erupting farts, your Viking name would be James the Eruptor.

HOW TO PLAY POOHSTICKS

1. Find at least one other person to compete against.
2. Collect some sticks of all shapes and sizes.
3. Find a small footbridge over a stream.
4. Select a stick and compare it with those belonging to the other competitors to make sure you can tell them apart.
5. Stand side by side on the bridge facing upstream.
6. Secretly check for fast-moving currents or slow, reedy areas and trapped logs.
7. On the count of three, drop (don't throw) your sticks into the water.
8. Quickly cross to the downstream side of the bridge and watch for the sticks to emerge.
9. The owner of the first stick to float out from under the bridge is the winner.

MAGIC WORDS

Abracadabra • Hocus pocus • Open sesame

Izzy wizzy let's get busy • Ala-kazham

SPY SPEAK

What you say: 'It is raining in St Petersburg.'
What you mean: 'The teacher is listening.'

What you say: 'The geese are heading north for the winter.'
What you mean: 'Meet me in the usual place after school.'

What you say: 'The roses are beautiful in Moscow this spring.'
What you mean: 'This is the person I fancy.'

What you say: 'The trains in Berlin always run on time.'
What you mean: 'Please cover for me.'

THE EQUATOR

The equator is an imaginary line that goes around the Earth halfway between the poles, dividing the planet into a northern and a southern hemisphere. It is about 40,000km (25,000 miles) long.

There are 13 countries on the equator:

São Tomé and Príncipe • Gabon • Kenya

Republic of Maldives • Indonesia • Kiribati • Ecuador

Democratic Republic of Congo • The Republic of Congo

Uganda • Somalia • Colombia • Brazil

————————HOW TO FIND ORION————————

The constellation Orion, the Hunter, can be seen all over the world because it lies on the celestial equator. Even if you haven't identified them in the night sky, you may have heard of some of the stars that make up this constellation, including Rigel and Betelgeuse.

1. Look towards the south if you are in the northern hemisphere, or north if you are in the southern hemisphere.

2. Find Orion's belt – three stars in a short, straight line.

3. Look for Orion's knee to the lower right – it's the bright star, Rigel.

4. Locate the orange-red star, Betelgeuse, at the upper left from the belt, which is often called 'Beetlejuice'.

5. Scan the sky farther away to the lower left of the belt for the brightest star in the sky: the Dog Star, Sirius.

————————BODILY FLUIDS————————

Pus is made of dead bacteria and dead blood cells

Bogeys are made mostly of sugars; that is why they taste so nice

You have 250,000 pores on your feet, which produce a quarter of a cup of sweat every day

You spray about 300 droplets of spit a minute when you are talking

——CAT WORDS——

Catalogue

Catapult

Category

Catastrophe

Catamaran

——RAT WORDS——

Ratatouille

Ratbag

Rattle

Ratatat

Ratify

POPCORN

Every kernel of popcorn contains a tiny amount of water.
When a kernel is heated, this water turns to steam.
The pressure grows until... 'pop!' – the kernel explodes
with a rush of steam. The kernel turns inside out and the
inside expands like white foam.

The first popcorn was made by Native Americans and
flavoured with herbs and spices. According to folklore the
popping sound was made by angry corn spirits that burst
out when the kernels became too hot to live in.

The average popping temperature for popcorn
is 175°C (347°F).

A water content of 13.5 per cent produces the ideal pop.

Popcorn has been served in cinemas since 1912.

The average American consumes about 51 litres (11 gallons, or
about 22 microwave popcorn bags) of popcorn every year.

Kernels that fail to pop are known as 'old maids'.

POPCORN FLAVOURS

Salt • Sugar • Caramel • Toffee • Curry
Cherry • Chilli • Cinnamon • Double chocolate
Coconut • Hot mustard • Nacho cheese

HALLOWEEN

In pagan times it was thought that the veil separating the worlds
of humans and their gods became thin at the onset of winter. It
was believed that on the festival of Samhain (31 October) the
gods came to Earth and played evil tricks. Fearful people lit
bonfires and made sacrifices in the hope that the gods would
leave them alone during this perilous time. Today we call this
festival Halloween.

——HOW TO TALK LIKE A PIRATE – BEGINNERS——

'Ahoy shipmates!'
'Hello everyone.'

'Aye!'
'Yes, I agree.'

'Aye aye!'
'I'm right on that!'

'Avast!'
'Stop!'

'Arrr!'
*Grunt used to fill
pauses in conversation.*

————————BEE COLONIES————————

A honeybee hive contains thousands of bees of three
different types: the queen, the workers and the drones.

THE QUEEN

A specially nurtured female that emerges from the hive and
mates with about 20 drones. She spends the next two years
of her life laying eggs.

THE WORKERS

Females that develop from fertilized eggs to make the
honey, build and guard the hive, tend the eggs, feed the
larvae, and raise the next queen. Workers are sterile,
and cannot reproduce.

THE DRONES

Stingless males bred from unfertilized eggs purely to mate
with the queen. In the process of mating, their vital organs
are ripped out and they die. Any drones that don't die in
this way are massacred by the workers, or turfed out
of the hive to starve or die of cold.

COUNTRY-FAIR SPORTS

JINGLING MATCH
A dozen blindfolded people move around within a roped-off ring. A man enters the ring without a blindfold, but with a bell around his neck and both hands tied behind him. The blindfolded men have to catch him.

SHIN KICKING
Athletes wearing iron-tipped boots kick each other in the shins. The first person to fall over twice loses.

FOOT WRESTLING
Two players lie on their backs on a wooden board with the soles of their feet touching. The object is to push the opponent off the board.

GREASY POLE
A greased telegraph pole is suspended over water with a flag at the furthest end. Players take it in turns to try to climb along the pole and reach the flag without falling into the water.

THE ABC OF LIFE-SAVING

A is for Airway
Check it is open and not blocked.

B is for Breathing
Make sure it is even and regular.

C is for Circulation
Check for a pulse to make sure blood is circulating around the body.

REAL ROCK STAR REQUESTS

'I want a bowl of M&Ms with all the brown ones removed.'

'All my food must be wrapped in clear plastic.'

'I want the seven dwarves up here now!'

'My coffee always has to be stirred anti-clockwise.'

'I want my hotel napkins personalized with my initials.'

'I want a dimmer switch in my dressing room.'

'I want bunny rabbits and kittens backstage
to keep me company.'

SLEEPY ANIMALS

Animal	Hours asleep per day
Koala	22
Little brown bat	19
Python	18
Tiger	15.8
Three-toed sloth	14.4
Cat	12
Human	8
Indian elephant	4
Horse	3
Giraffe	2

A SONG THAT GETS ON EVERYBODY'S NERVES

'I know a song that gets on everybody's nerves.
I know a song that gets on everybody's nerves.
I know a song that gets on everybody's nerves.
And this is how it goes...'
[Repeat forever]

────── THE WORLD'S COOLEST BUNGEE JUMPS ──────

CLIFTON SUSPENSION BRIDGE (England)
The Oxford Dangerous Sports Club invented
the modern bungee jump on 1 April 1978. The
first ever bungee jump was from the 76-m
(249-ft) Clifton Suspension Bridge.

BLOUKRANS RIVER BRIDGE (South Africa)
This is the world's highest commercial bungee
jump. Jumpers experience a seven-second
free fall from the 216-m (708-ft) bridge.

THE 'GOLDENEYE' DAM
(Switzerland-Italy border)
In the 1995 film *GoldenEye*, James Bond
bungee-jumps over the edge of a dam
in Russia. This dam is in fact on
the Swiss-Italian border, but the
stunt was genuine.

────── BORED OF BUNGEE JUMPS? TRY THESE! ──────

BUNGEE DROP
This is the same as a
bungee jump except that
you cut the cord just
before springing back up
from the ground, and
touch down safely.

THE CATAPULT
You start on the ground and
the bungee cord is stretched
from wherever it is fixed.
When released, this pulls
you up into the air at
great speed.

BUNGEE TRAMPOLINE
You are suspended in a
harness from bungee cords
that let you jump much
higher than you normally
could on a trampoline.

BRIDGE SWING
You free-fall from a bridge
and then swing backwards
and forwards in a long,
high-speed arc (instead of
bouncing up and down
as you would in a
bungee jump).

──── A QUICK GUIDE TO WESTERN PHILOSOPHY ────

EXISTENTIALISM
Life has no deeper meaning so I am free to act as I choose. On the other hand, since life has no meaning, I might as well not bother doing anything.

MATERIALISM
Only physical things truly exist. Everything else, such as love or anger or a belief in God, can be explained in physical terms.

FATALISM
Everything that is going to happen is already decided and I have no free will. Since everything will happen the same, no matter what I do, I might as well do nothing.

RELATIVISM
There is no right and wrong, and no good and evil. There are only judgements that we agree on.

SOLIPSISM
I am real and so are my experiences, but I can't be sure that anything else exists.

EMPIRICISM
True knowledge comes through practical experience, not thought.

POSTMODERNISM
There is nothing that is true for the whole of humanity. We are therefore free to invent and practise our own philosophies.

──────────── INUIT WORDS FOR SNOW ────────────

Iñupiaq is a language spoken by Iñupiaq Inuits in Alaska. Here are some of their words for snow:

Aniuvak	A mound of packed snow
Apun	Fallen snow
Nutaġaq	Fresh powder snow
Piqsiq	Wet snow
Pukak	Granular snow formed under another layer
Qaŋattaaq	Overhanging snow
Qannik	Falling snow
Silliq	Crusty, hard snow

LEGALLY BLIND

A legally blind person has to stand 6m (20ft) away from an object to see it with the same degree of clarity as a normally sighted person can from 61m (200ft), even when wearing the best glasses.

TRADITIONAL CAKES

Pumpkin pie...USA

Moon cake..China

Victoria sponge..England

Poppyseed cake...Poland

Pavlova..New Zealand

Lady fingers...France

Cheesecake...Ancient Greece

Black Forest gateau..Germany

Due to the nature of infinity, an infinite number of monkeys randomly hitting the keys of a typewriter will eventually type out the complete works of William Shakespeare.

MISSING TREASURE

THE CROWN JEWELS OF MARIE ANTOINETTE
In 1792, the jewels of the beheaded French queen Marie Antoinette were stolen by revolutionaries. The Sancy Diamond and French Blue Diamond were never recovered.

KING JOHN'S TREASURE
The King of England lost his treasure, including the Crown Jewels, when horses pulling a carriage containing the treasure got disorientated in a swirling fog. They dragged the treasure carriage into a murky stretch of water.

NAZI GOLD
During the Second World War, Nazis in Germany looted foreigners' treasure. Gold was transferred into top-secret Swiss banks and never heard of again.

THE KNIGHTS' TEMPLAR TREASURE
This powerful order of medieval knights were thought to have been the guardians of the Holy Grail. To this day the Grail's whereabouts allegedly remains a closely guarded secret.

Chinese gooseberries come from New Zealand.

HOW TO TALK LIKE A PIRATE – ADVANCED

'The Sun be over the yardarm, 'tis time for victuals, and smartly, me hearty!'
'It's getting late – hurry up with dinner, I'm starving, mate!'

'Let's see what's crawled out of the bunghole.'
'Let's see what's for dinner.'

'Bring me a noggin of rum, now, won't you, matey?'
'Can I have a drink?'

'The cat's out of the bag, the wind's gone out of me sails, and I'll be swinging from the yardarm afore eight bells.'
'I'm in big trouble.'

NOT-SO-SECRET DIARIES

THE SECRET DIARY OF ADRIAN MOLE, AGED 13³/₄
Written by Sue Townsend, this diary of Adrian Mole (there are now six) tells of an English teenage boy's growing pains.

THE DIARY OF SAMUEL PEPYS
This 17th-century Londoner wrote his diaries in a code that wasn't cracked until long after his death. He wrote about the things he saw first-hand, including the Great Fire of London and public executions.

THE DIARY OF ANNE FRANK
Anne Frank was a Jewish Dutch girl who went into hiding from the Nazis during the Second World War. She kept a diary for the two years that she spent in a secret annex of a house.

CAPTAIN SCOTT'S JOURNAL
Robert Falcon Scott kept a diary of his team's expedition to the South Pole in 1912. He and four others died shortly after reaching the Pole.

HOW TO BECOME A SAINT

1. Die. In Roman Catholicism, you cannot usually become a saint until at least five years after your death.

2. Local bishops must investigate your life, and send their findings to the Pope.

3. The Pope proclaims you are a virtuous role model.

4. Two verifiable miracles must occur because of you. (Officially, a miracle must involve no trickery and must also suspend the laws of nature.)

The worst Viking vengeance was known as the 'Blood-Red Eagle'. The enemy's back was cut open, his ribs were pulled from his spine and his lungs were removed.

——THE WORLD'S LONGEST STARING CONTEST——

——————OXYMORONS——————

Oxymorons are words that are used together that have contradictory meanings. They don't make any sense, but they make complete sense.

Living dead

Seriously funny

Same difference

Virtual reality

Almost exactly

Deafening silence

Clearly confused

——————SIXTH SENSE——————

Intuition...A gut feeling about something

Déjà vu..........................The feeling of having seen something before

Telepathy.........The ability to pass thoughts from person to person

Medium................Someone who can sense the presence of spirits

Visionary....A person who can see into the future through dreams

Mind-reading............................Tuning in to another person's thoughts

NATURAL HAIRSTYLES

Widow's peak...........................V-shaped point in middle of forehead

Cowlick....................Swirl of unruly hair that can't be combed down

Crown...................................A whorl of hair at the centre of the scalp

Double crown............Two whorls of hair at the centre of the scalp

HOW FAR CAN YOU SEE?

ON A CLEAR DAY
As far as the Sun, 150 million km (93 million miles) away

ON A CLEAR NIGHT
As far as the Andromeda Galaxy, 2 million light years away
(one light year is 9.5 million million km (nearly
6 million million miles))

WITH THE BEST TELESCOPE
14 billion light years away

The fastest speed ever reached on a
skateboard was 100.6kph (62.5mph). The
skater was Gary Hardwick of California, USA.

HEALING CRYSTALS

Amethyst...Peace and harmony

Carnelian...Focus

Citrine..Mental clarity

Quartz..Energy and healing

Amber..Digestion and reproduction

Tiger's eye...Well-being and confidence

Tourmaline..Purity and protection

──────── ALLEGED MERMAID SIGHTINGS ────────

ENGLAND, 1167
A merman was
washed up onto the
beach at Orford,
Suffolk. He was kept
in Orford Castle for
six months before
escaping back
into the sea.

POLAND, 1531
A mermaid caught by fishermen in the Baltic Sea was sent
to the King of Poland. She died after three days in captivity.

CEYLON, 1560
Seven merpeople were spotted by passengers on board
a boat bound for India, off the west coast of Ceylon (now
Sri Lanka). Witnesses included the Viceroy of Goa.

IRELAND, 1819
A young mermaid was caught off the Irish coast. She was the
size of a ten-year-old child with long hair and dark eyes. A boy
shot at her with a gun and she disappeared back into the sea.

──── THE YOSEMITE SYSTEM OF MOUNTAINEERING ────

The Yosemite system of mountaineering grades the
difficulty of climbing routes.

Class 1..Hiking

Class 2....................Simple scrambling with occasional use of hands

Class 3.................................Scrambling with occasional aid of a rope

Class 4..........Simple climbing with exposure and possible fatal falls

Class 5...Technical free climbing

Class 6.........................Artificial or aid climbing; for example, climbing
a rope up a sheer face with no holds

―――――――DO-IT-YOURSELF HUMAN BEINGS―――――――

GOLEM

In Jewish folklore, a golem was a human-like creature made of clay and brought to life by a holy man. The Golem could not speak and would perform tasks for the holy man. Often he would cause trouble by taking a task too literally.

FRANKENSTEIN'S MONSTER

In Mary Shelley's novel *Frankenstein*, the Swiss scientist Dr Frankenstein creates a monster out of body parts taken from local graveyards and dissecting rooms. The monster wreaks havoc after he is shunned by the horrified doctor.

HOMUNCULUS

According to the 15th-century Austrian alchemist Paracelsus, a homunculus was a human-like being made in the warmth of horse manure and nourished by human blood. Marvellous creatures such as pygmies, woodsprites and giants were all homunculi.

PINOCCHIO

In the children's story by the Italian author Carlo Collodi, a wooden puppet made by the childless carpenter Geppetto comes to life. After proving his worth, the puppet, called Pinocchio, is magically turned into a real boy.

―――――――FEATS OF―――――――
GREAT STRENGTH

Performing one-fingered press-ups
Ripping up a telephone directory
Bending a steel bar
Breaking metal chains
Lifting a car
Pushing a bus with your head
Pulling a Boeing 747

THE COLOUR OF NOISE

If sound waves are translated into light waves, different sounds appear as different colours.

Sound waves	Light waves
TV static, urban traffic	White
Rushing water or ocean surf	Pink
Subway train, noisy air-conditioning system	Red
Roomful of five-year-olds playing recorders	Orange
Piercing hiss	Blue
Random footsteps	Brown
Natural background noise	Green
Silence	Black

Identical twins usually die within three years of each other.

UNLIKELY PARTNERSHIPS

THE CLOWN FISH AND THE SEA ANEMONE
The clown fish is immune to the anemone's stinging tentacles. It keeps the anemone's tentacles clean and in return is protected from predators.

THE ANT AND THE CATERPILLAR
Some Australian caterpillars have special glands that produce a honey-like liquid that ants like to drink. In return, the ants protect the defenceless caterpillar from parasites.

THE PILOT FISH AND THE SHARK
Tiny pilot fish swim into sharks' mouths and nibble away any rotting food caught between the sharks' teeth. Sharks rarely eat these swimming toothpicks, and instead help them by scaring off would-be predators.

THE KNIGHTS' CODE

Rescue damsels in distress

Love your country

Defend your monarch

Respect your fellow knights

Never refuse a challenge

Don't hide from your enemies

Live honourably and fight for glory

Give to the poor

Protect the weak

Stand up against injustice

Don't tell lies

Always finish what you begin

HOW TO RECOGNIZE A WITCH

According to the children's author Roald Dahl, witches dress and look just like normal women. A witch might even live next door to you, or work in your local shop, or be the headmistress of your school. Luckily there are ways to spot a witch:

They wear gloves because they have claws that need hiding.

They are bald and wear wigs.

They have larger nose holes than ordinary people.

The black dot in the middle of their eyes changes colour from fire to ice.

They don't have toes, so they have to wear wide shoes with square ends.

They have blue spit.

INTERESTING BRIDGES

BRIDGE OF SIGHS, VENICE, ITALY
Prisoners crossed this bridge before being taken to their cells.
It is said they would sigh as they took their last view of Venice.

LONDON BRIDGE, LONDON, ENGLAND
Until 1750 this was the only bridge over the River Thames.
Heads of traitors were placed on spikes above the
southern gate of the bridge.

MILLAU BRIDGE, MASSIF CENTRAL MOUNTAINS, FRANCE
343m (1,125ft) tall at its highest point, this bridge is
taller than the Eiffel Tower.

THE FORTH RAIL BRIDGE, QUEENSFERRY, SCOTLAND
This Victorian bridge is so long that, until recent developments
in paint technology, it had to be continuously painted — as
soon as the people painting it had got to the end, it was time
to start at the beginning again!

GOLDEN GATE BRIDGE, SAN FRANCISCO, USA
When it was built in 1937, this was the largest suspension
bridge in the world. Today the Akashi Kaikyo Bridge in
Japan holds that title.

MATHEMATICAL BRIDGE, CAMBRIDGE, ENGLAND
Rumoured to have been designed by Sir Isaac Newton
without the use of nuts or bolts to hold the wood together.
According to legend, students dismantled the bridge one
night, but were unable to put it back together. It was
then rebuilt using nuts and bolts.

COOL GADGETS

Bulletproof jacket • Lock-picking kit • Micro-tracers
Grappling hook • Wrist radio • Smokescreen pellets
Anti-puncture bike tyres • Infrared specs
Anti-gravity hovering skateboard
Super-strong rope contained in a yo-yo

──────THE WORLD'S SIMPLEST CARD TRICK──────

1. Shuffle the deck in front of a friend.

2. Secretly peek at the card on the bottom and remember it.

3. Ask your friend to pick a card, any card, from the deck and look at it carefully without showing you.

4. Cut the cards — take the top half of the deck in your left hand and the bottom half in your right hand.

5. Hold out the left-hand pile and tell your friend to put their card on top of it.

6. Put the cards from your right hand on top of the pile.

7. You can now work through the pack, card by card, until you come to the card originally on the bottom of the pack. Your friend's card is the next one, but go past it so that it looks like you've missed it.

8. Return to the correct card and sit back as your friend stares at you in awe and amazement.

──────────HOW LOUD IS A DECIBEL?──────────

0 decibels..Threshold of hearing

10..Human breathing

15..Whisper

80..Vacuum cleaner

90..Loud factory (harmful)

120..Rock concert

130..Train horn

150..Rifle firing

180..Blue whale humming

250............................Inside a tornado (death to humans)

A WARNING TO PIRATES

The notorious British pirate Captain Kidd was hanged at Execution Dock in London on 23 May 1701. On the first attempt, the rope broke, so Kidd was strung up and hanged again. His body was suspended in the sea and left for the tide to wash over it three times. Then it was painted in tar, bound in chains and hung up in a metal cage. His rotting corpse served as a warning to pirates sailing in and out of London.

SWITCHING ON A LIGHT

The speed of light is approximately 300,000km per second (186,000 miles per second). If you could slow this down to 1m per second you would be able to see the way shadows are gradually chased away when you turn on a light:

You flick the light switch. For a while nothing happens.

After a few seconds the light bulb gradually begins to light up, but the room remains completely dark.

Slowly a sphere of light begins to spread around the bulb, creating a halo effect. Gradually the sphere of light expands to fill the room.

The room is now completely illuminated, apart from the shadows which remain pitch black.

Light bouncing off the walls begins to fill the shadows, and eventually they start to lighten.

You switch off the light. The shadows are the last areas to return to pitch black.

—HOW TO RIP A TELEPHONE DIRECTORY IN HALF—

1. With the spine of the book towards you, place your hands on top of the book and grip it with your little and ring fingers. Bend the book into a U shape by pushing with your thumbs.

2. Now hold the book tightly with all your fingers and bend the ends of the book down. The pages will form a V shape.

3. As you continue to bend the edges of the book down, the pages will start to split.

4. Push with one of your hands and pull with the other to rip the book in half.

The world record for ripping up telephone directories is held by Ed Shelton of the USA. On 18 November 2005 he ripped up 55 directories from top to bottom in three minutes.

THE GAME

The Game is a mental game. The aim of The Game is to forget that you are playing it. As many players as you want can play. Players only need to be aware of a few simple rules:

1. To know of The Game's existence is to play The Game.

2. To realize you have thought of The Game is to lose The Game.

3. When you lose, you must immediately announce, 'I have lost The Game.'

4. If anyone present asks 'What is The Game?' you must explain these rules.

5. Other players of The Game who are present when you announce that you have lost have a 30-minute grace period in which to forget about The Game before they also lose.

6. It is not possible to know that you have won The Game, only to have won it and remain ignorant of the fact.

THE HIGHEST MOUNTAINS ON MARS

Olympus Mons..27km (16.8 miles)

Ascraeus Mons..11km (6.8 miles)

Arsia Mons..9km (5.6 miles)

Pavonis Mons..7km (4.3 miles)

Alba Patera..3km (1.9 miles)

The highest mountain on Earth is Mount Everest, which is 8.85km (5.5 miles) high.

RUSSIAN SPACE DOGS

Laika • Belka • Strelaka
Chernushka • Veterok
Ugolyok

AMERICAN SPACE MONKEYS

Albert • Gordo • Able
Baker • Sam • Bonny
Scatback

——SUPERHEROES YOU PROBABLY DON'T KNOW——

ULTRAMAN (Japan)
132ft- (40m-) tall alien from Nebula M78. He can fly at seven times the speed of sound and can only spend three minutes on Earth at a time.

STIG (Canada)
An undead spirit, Stig was attacked by demons and woke to find himself in Hell. Mistaken for Satan in disguise, he became leader of the Underworld, with the ability to send bolts of fire from his hands.

EL BULBO (Mexico)
Brought to life when a spell was cast on the bulbs in a television set, El Bulbo is a superhero who fights his arch-rival and fellow light bulb Adolfo. He can fly, grow to an enormous size and fire destructive rays.

NAGRAJ (India)
Microscopic snakes living in his bloodstream give him superhuman strength, a venomous bite and snakes that shoot out of his wrists.

> Scientists think it likely that the universe was created 13.7 billion years ago.

——————REVOLUTIONS——————

AMERICAN REVOLUTION
The 13 colonies of America broke away from Great Britain and became a republic of united states, 1774—83

FRENCH REVOLUTION
Overthrow of the French monarchy and aristocracy and the establishment of a French republic, 1789—99

RUSSIAN REVOLUTION
Abdication of Czar Nicholas II and the establishment of Soviet Union, 1917

VELVET REVOLUTION
Bloodless overthrow of Communist government in Czechoslovakia, 1989

FENCING TERMS

A bout..A fencing match

Salute.............A courteous gesture at the start and finish of a bout

Allee!..The command to begin

Parry...A defensive stroke

Riposte...A counter-attack after a parry

Esquive.............................Ducking or side-stepping to avoid being hit

Pattinando...A lunge

Coulé...A glide

Prise de fer...Taking the opponent's blade

Finale...........................The last move in a series of attacking actions

PANGRAMS

Pangrams are sentences that contain every letter of
the alphabet at least once.

The quick brown fox jumps over the lazy dog.

The five boxing wizards jump quickly.

Five or six jet planes zoomed quickly by the tower.

————————FREE-RUNNING MOVES————————

Free running is usually practised in urban areas and is a way of moving through the environment fluidly. Free runners use a series of vaults, jumps and athletic movements to pass through, over and under everyday obstacles such as stairs, rails and walls.

Wall climb...Scaling a vertical surface

Underbar..Jumping or swinging through a gap

Gap jump....................................Jumping from one location to another

Turn vault.....................................Vaulting to the other side of an object

Tic tac....................................Kicking off one surface to clear another

Rail precision..Jumping from one rail to another

Cat balance.................................Running on hands and feet along a
rail or narrow surface

————————THE FIVE KINGDOMS OF LIVING THINGS————————

Monerans   Organisms with simple cell structures; for
example, bacteria.

Protists   Simple organisms with nuclei and other complex
cell structures; for example, some algae.

Fungi   Primitive plants that decompose dead plant and
animal matter; for example, mushrooms and yeast.

Plants   Multicellular organisms, usually with cell walls
composed mainly of cellulose. Plants typically
use sunlight as an energy source, and convert
light energy, water and carbon dioxide into
glucose, oxygen and water through a process
called photosynthesis.

Animals   Multicellular organisms that feed on other
organisms. Almost all animals can respond to
changes in their environment by moving all or
part of their bodies.

A KNIGHTLY TOURNAMENT

JOUST
Knights on horseback charge at each other with long lances under their arms. The aim is to knock your opponent off his horse.

MELÉE A PIED
Knights fight on foot with blunted swords. You win if you strike your opponent three times.

ARCHERY
Knights shoot 12 arrows at the centre of a target, scoring points for accuracy. The best shot wins.

WRESTLING
Knights fight unarmed and the winner is decided by the best of five throws.

REALLY STUPID

A woman in Texas, USA, had bought a new car and wanted to check out the size of the boot. She asked her family members to shut her inside it, then realized she was still holding the keys.

While out hunting in Arizona, USA, a man accidentally shot himself in the leg. To try to attract the attention of someone who could rescue him, he fired his gun a second time. Unfortunately he shot himself in the other leg.

A shopkeeper in Texas, USA, accepted a fake $100 bill even though it was over a foot long.

Some British soldiers, who were standing in for the fire service during a strike in 1978, were called to help an old lady rescue her cat from a tree. Mission accomplished, she invited them in for some tea and biscuits. Afterwards, the soldiers waved goodbye, got in their vehicle and ran over the cat.

———TRACKING FOOTPRINTS———

Grizzly bear   Duck   Beaver

Wild pig   Hedgehog   Monster

———WAVE HEIGHT SCALE———

Glassy..0m (0ft)
Rippled...0.3—0.6m (1—2ft)
Choppy..0.6—1.2m (2—4ft)
Very rough..4—6m (13—20ft)
Mid-ocean storm waves..6—9m (20—30ft)
Extreme waves..15m—30m (50—100ft)
Freak waves...30m+ (100ft+)

——THE WORLD'S MOST DANGEROUS ANIMALS——

POLAR BEAR
Found only in the Arctic, the polar bear is the largest land carnivore, and is twice the size of a tiger. It hunts both on land and in the sea, camouflaged white against the snow. When food is scarce, polar bears may kill and eat humans.

GREAT WHITE SHARK
Up to 6m (20ft) long and weighing over 2,000kg (4,400lb), the great white shark is the world's largest predatory fish. Great whites ambush their prey by swimming up from the bottom of the sea. They have extra rows of teeth behind their main ones that are constantly growing. Their teeth are retractable, like a cat's claws.

BOX JELLYFISH
Also known as the sea wasp, this cube-shaped jellyfish is only found in tropical seas. Its tentacles unleash fast-working venom that can shut down a human victim's heart and lungs in as little as three minutes. Kills more people every year than any other sea creature.

FUNNEL-WEB SPIDER
The world's most deadly spider comes from Australia, where it likes to live in cool, sheltered habitats. The males are known to bite aggressively and repeatedly. Death can occur any time from 15 minutes to 3 days after the bite.

INLAND TAIPAN SNAKE
Found in Central Australia, this snake has 12mm- (0.5in-) long fangs. It has the most lethal venom in the world, and one bite contains enough poison to kill several adult humans.

KOMODO DRAGON
The largest lizard in the world, the Komodo dragon hunts live prey on the island of Komodo in Indonesia. Deadly bacteria in the dragon's mouth quickly kill a bitten victim.

KILLER BEES
These extremely aggressive bees have a tendency to swarm. They have a high proportion of soldier bees that guard their hive, and pursue and sting perceived threats over long distances.

REAL CRAYON COLOURS

Magenta	Tan	Sea green
Pink sherbert	Wheat	Aquamarine
Crimson	Moccasin	Turquoise
Tomato	Almond	Cyan
Coral	Khaki	Teal
Salmon	Dandelion	Azure
Indian red	Lemon yellow	Sky blue
Fire brick	Gold	Navy
Maroon	Spring green	Midnight blue
Chocolate	Lawn green	Slate blue
Sienna	Lime	Cornflower blue
Sunset Orange	Olive	Royal blue
Apricot	Forest	Steel blue
Goldenrod	Jungle green	Orchid

TECTONIC PLATES

The Earth's crust is made up of slabs of rock, known as tectonic plates, that are in constant motion.

African Plate	Juan de Fuca Plate
Antarctic Plate	Nazca Plate
Arabian Plate	North American Plate
Australian Plate	Pacific Plate
Caribbean Plate	Philippine Plate
Cocos Plate	Scotia Plate
Eurasian Plate	South American Plate
Indian Plate	

SERVING PLATES

Plates from which food is served or eaten.

Dinner plate
Saucer
Side plate
Platter
Spinning plate
Trencher
Paper plate
Ashet

──THE OFFICIAL ROUTE TO DRACULA'S CASTLE──

Day One: Catch the 8.35 pm overnight train from Munich in Bavaria to the Austrian capital Vienna, arriving at 6.46 am.

Day Two: After breakfasting in Vienna, take the early train to the Hungarian capital Budapest. There, catch a connecting train, arriving at nightfall in the Transylvanian town of Klausenburgh, also known as Cluj-Napoca. Stay the night at the Hotel Royale.

Day Three: Take the 7.55 am train to the northern Transylvanian city of Bistritz, also known as Bistrita. Arrive at dusk and stay at the Golden Krone Hotel, recommended by Count Dracula.

Day Four: Accept the crucifix given to you by the fearful hotelier when he discovers you are travelling to Dracula's Castle. Take the early-morning stagecoach to Bukovinia, on the north-eastern slopes of the Carpathian Mountains of Transylvania.

Day Five: At precisely midnight you will be dropped on the Borgo Pass, a lonely road that runs into the heart of the mountains. After a terrifying wait in the dark, a horseman will meet you and take you through a wolf-infested forest and blizzarding snow to Castle Dracula.

──ANIMALS THAT GIVE BIRTH TO CALVES──

Buffalos · Elephants · Cows · Giraffes · Hippopotamuses
Moose · Camels · Antelopes · Elk · Whales · Dolphins

FAMOUS EQUATIONS

THE DEFINITION OF PI

Pi (π) is the ratio of the length of a circle's outer edge (circumference) to the distance across its centre (diameter). It is always the same, regardless of the size of the circle, and is roughly equal to 3.141592653.

$$\pi = \frac{c}{d}$$

π = pi
c = circumference of the circle
d = diameter of the circle

EINSTEIN'S THEORY OF RELATIVITY

Albert Einstein discovered that when an object has a mass, it has an amount of energy related to that mass. The following equation works on the principle that the resting energy of an object is equal to its mass multiplied by the square of the speed of light:

$$E = mc^2$$

E = energy
m = mass
c = the speed of light

NEWTON'S GRAVITY LAW

Every object which has mass (weight) also has a gravitational pull. The larger the object, the stronger the pull. Every object, therefore, attracts every other object with a gravitational force that is proportional to each of their masses and the distance between them:

$$F = \frac{Gm_1m_2}{d^2}$$

F = force of gravitational attraction between two masses (m_1 and m_2)
G = gravitational constant (the force of gravity that is constantly present)
d = distance between the two masses

PYTHAGORAS' THEOREM

In a right-angled triangle, the sum of the squares of the two shortest sides is equal to the square of the longest side:

$$a^2 + b^2 = c^2$$

a = short side of a right-angled triangle
b = other short side of a right-angled triangle
c = long side of a right-angle triangle

——TIGHTROPE FEATS OF THE GREAT BLONDIN——

The Great Blondin was the greatest daredevil ever to cross the Niagara Falls. On 30 June 1859 he walked on a tightrope over the Falls. When he got to the centre he lowered a rope to a boat below, pulled up a bottle and sat down on his tightrope for a drink. He went on to perform the following amazing feats over the huge waterfall:

cooking an omelette

riding a bicycle

doing a backwards somersault

walking with his hands and feet tied

walking blindfolded

pushing a wheelbarrow

carrying his manager on his back

——————HOW FAST IS STANDING STILL?——————

The Earth is spinning around the Sun at approximately 112,000kph (70,000mph). Meanwhile, the solar system is travelling through space at 273km per second (170 miles per second).

——HOW MANY TO CHANGE A LIGHT BULB?——

Owls...................................None. Owls aren't afraid of the dark.

Martians...One and a half.

Monkeys......................Three. One to change the light bulb, and two to throw bananas at each other.

Poltergeists.............................Two. One to hold the light bulb and the other to twist the room around.

STREET ART YOU CAN DO

Do five press-ups and have a friend count really loudly:
'996, 997, 998, 999, 1,000!'

Juggle uncooked eggs but keep dropping them.

Follow passers-by and impersonate the way they walk.

Sing out of tune through a traffic cone.

Talk to an imaginary person trapped down a grate.

Stand on a box and clear your throat as if you are about
to sing. Then clear your throat some more, and just
keep on clearing your throat.

Pretend you have jelly legs, and keep wobbling and falling
over and getting up and falling over again.

Draw ugly portraits of passers-by.

BAD LUCK AT THE THEATRE

Whistling or clapping backstage.

Saying '*Macbeth*'. (Instead, say 'The Scottish play.')

Wishing someone good luck. (Instead, say 'Break a leg.')

Turning off the light when the stage is not in use.

——MAGICAL BEASTS IN HARRY POTTER NOVELS——

HIPPOGRIFF
Beast of the air and of the ground, it has the head and wings of a giant eagle and the body of a horse. A stickler for the formalities of good manners, the hippogriff will be irritable if bows are not exchanged by way of greeting.

CENTAUR
Supremely intelligent being with the head and torso of a human and the body of a horse. Equally mistrustful of muggles and wizards, they live in deep forests.

HUNGARIAN HORNTAIL
Scaly, black dragon with yellow eyes. Frequent jets of flame are fired from its jaws and a blow from its spiked tail can be deadly.

WEREWOLF
When the Moon is full, this otherwise perfectly reasonable human turns into a bloodthirsty beast. The curse is caught from the bite of another werewolf, and there is no known cure. Werewolves are to be pitied, but not at close range on the night of a full Moon.

DOXY
Tiny, winged creature with four legs, four arms and a thick covering of black fur. They have venomous teeth and a deadly bite.

BASILISK
Venomous-fanged serpent with a deadly stare. Illegally produced by hatching a chicken's egg under a toad.

——THE THREE OFFICIAL TYPES OF FREAK WAVE——

WALL OF WATER
A wave that is preceded by a deep trough known as a 'hole in the sea' and travels up to 10km (6 miles) through the ocean.

THREE SISTERS
Groups of three huge waves.

GIANT STORM WAVE
A single wave that builds to up to four times the normal height of a storm wave, then collapses after a few seconds.

ANIMAL DEFENCES

BADGERS
The skin on a badger's bottom is so baggy that if a predator gets its teeth into it, the badger is able to twist round and bite back.

RABBITS
A rabbit's eyes are set on the sides of its head. This increases the rabbit's field of vision and allows it to keep watch for predators, even while eating.

IO MOTHS
When threatened, these moths pull back their upper wings to reveal markings like a pair of eyes. This startles the attacker and gives the moth time to escape.

PUFFER FISH
These unusual fish can inflate themselves to several times their normal size by swallowing water or air.

HEDGEHOGS
When threatened by predators, hedgehogs roll up into a ball of prickles.

SKUNKS
Skunks spray a sticky and foul-smelling fluid at predators. The stench is strong enough to put off even the hardiest bear.

HOMONYMS

Homonyms are words that sound the same, but are spelt differently and have different meanings.

Carat — Carrot	Plain — Plane
Ate — Eight	Some — Sum
Quay — Key	For — Four
Wait — Weight	You — Ewe
Dear — Deer	Pail — Pale
Knight — Night	Scent — Cent

EVERYDAY CONUNDRUMS

CATCH-22

Sometimes called a vicious circle, a Catch-22 is a situation in which you have to do one thing to achieve another, but you can't achieve the first thing until you've achieved the second:

> *'I can't make money from washing cars until I've bought the equipment I need, but I can't buy the equipment I need until I've made some money from washing cars.'*

MORTON'S FORK

A choice between two equally unpleasant alternatives:

> *'You can do your homework first and then clean your bedroom, or you can clean your bedroom first and then do your homework.'*

HOBSON'S CHOICE

An apparently free choice that is really no choice at all:

> *'You can have either of these two chocolates, as long as I can have that one.'*

FAMOUS NUMBERS

007...James Bond

666...The number of the Beast

2000..The second millennium, or Y2K

9-11...............The date of the terrorist attacks on New York in 2001

180.............................The highest possible score in the game of darts

13...Unlucky number

365...Days in a year (except leap years)

299,792,458...........................The speed of light in metres per second

$9\frac{3}{4}$.................................The train platform from which the Hogwart's Express departs in the *Harry Potter* books

80...........The number of days it takes to go around the world in Jules Verne's novel *Around The World In Eighty Days*

ASSASSINATED LEADERS

MOHANDAS K. GANDHI
A pacifist campaigner for Indian independence, Gandhi was shot three times by his enemy Nathuram Godse on 30 January 1948.

ARCHDUKE FRANZ FERDINAND
Franz Ferdinand was the heir to the throne of Austro-Hungary. His assassination by Gavrilo Princip on 28 June 1914 sparked the Second World War.

ABRAHAM LINCOLN
This President of the United States of America was assassinated on 14 April 1865 while watching a theatre performance. The assassin was John Wilkes Booth, who shot the President in the back of the head.

JOHN FITZGERALD KENNEDY
When this President of the United States of America was shot in the head on 22 November 1963, a man called Lee Harvey Oswald was accused. Many people believe that Oswald was either framed or part of a larger conspiracy.

JULIUS GAIUS CAESAR
On 15 March 44BC, the Roman Emperor Julius Caesar was stabbed 23 times while he slept in his bed. The assassination was carried out by a conspiracy of Roman senators, one of whom was Caesar's friend Brutus.

THE MINERAL HARDNESS SCALE

The Mohs scale is a system for classifying mineral hardness. Each mineral can make a scratch in those below it in the scale.

10. Diamond (hardest)
9. Corundum
8. Topaz
7. Quartz
6. Orthoclase
5. Apatite
4. Fluorite
3. Calcite
2. Gypsum
1. Talc (softest)

────────HOW TO READ TEA LEAVES────────

Drink a cup of leaf tea from a plain white cup and leave a small amount of liquid in the bottom. Hold the cup in your left hand and swirl the liquid around three times in a clockwise direction, making sure that the leaves reach the rim but don't spill over. Turn the cup upside down onto

a saucer, letting the liquid drain away. After seven seconds, turn the cup back the right way up and hold it so that the handle points towards you. You can use the patterns created to predict the future:

Acorn	Success will be yours
Bell	You will receive unexpected news
Cat	A friend will lie
Dagger	Beware of danger
Face	You will make a new friend
Goat	Beware of enemies
Harp	You will fall in love
Rabbit	You will need to be brave
Ship	You will go on a long journey
Tree	Good health will be yours
Wheel	You will get good exam results
Zebra	There will be a dramatic change in your life

────────────BIKES────────────

Quadracycle • Penny farthing • Unicycle • Tandem
Exercise bike • Racing bike • Mountain bike • BMX

————THE OFFICIAL RULES OF THE 'WORLD———— CHERRY PIT SPIT CHAMPIONSHIP'

1. Each cherry is put in the mouth whole and the flesh eaten before spitting the pit. The pit is the stone in the middle of the cherry.

2. The longest of three spits is recorded. If a pit is swallowed, that spit is forfeited.

3. No foreign objects may be held in the mouth that might give an advantage in spitting the pit.

4. No popping the cheeks. The spitter's hands must remain below the shoulders.

5. Contestants' feet may not touch or cross the foul line.

The longest recorded spit is 28.5m (93ft 6.5in).

An anaconda snake can eat a 2m- (6ft 7in-) long crocodile.

————————————CULTURAL SYMBOLS————————

COUNTRY	ANIMAL	FOOD
Germany	Black eagle	Sauerkraut
USA	Bald eagle / Bison	Hamburger
England	Lion / Bulldog	Fish and chips
Wales	Red dragon	Laver bread
Australia	Kangaroo	Barbecue
France	Rooster	Frogs' legs
Scotland	Red lion	Haggis
Spain	Bull	Paella / Tapas
Russia	Eagle / Bear	Borscht
Canada	Beaver	Maple syrup

THE STORY OF WEAPONS

2,500,000BC...Stone tools first used

6,000BC...Metal spears first thrown

2,000BC.........................Celtic tribes fight using horse-drawn chariots

400BC....................Ancient Greeks use ballistas (giant bolt throwers)

AD950...Chinese invent gunpowder

1128...Chinese first use cannons

1400...Shotguns first used

1914—18.........First World War — tanks first used instead of horses

1939—45.......................Second World War — assault rifles first used

1945............................Allies use the first atomic bombs against Japan

SHOOTING STARS

METEOROID
Space debris of all shapes and sizes

METEOR
The glowing trail of burning gas that occurs when a
meteoroid enters a planet's atmosphere and heats up

METEORITE
A meteoroid that hits the Earth

FAMOUS BEGINNINGS

'Once there were four children whose names were Peter, Susan, Edmund and Lucy.'
The Lion, the Witch and the Wardrobe by C. S. Lewis

'Alice was beginning to get very tired of sitting by her sister on the bank, and of having nothing to do: once or twice she had peeped into the book her sister was reading, but it had no pictures or conversations in it, "and what is the use of a book," thought Alice, "without pictures or conversations?"'
Alice's Adventures in Wonderland by Lewis Carroll

'Here is Edward Bear, coming downstairs now, bump, bump, bump, on the back of his head, behind Christopher Robin.'
Winnie-the-Pooh by A. A. Milne

'Mr and Mrs Dursley, of number four, Privet Drive, were proud to say that they were perfectly normal, thank you very much.'
Harry Potter and the Philosopher's Stone by J. K. Rowling

'Lyra and her daemon moved through the darkening Hall, taking care to keep to one side, out of sight of the kitchen.'
Northern Lights by Philip Pullman

PAPER SIZES

A0.......841x1189mm (33.1x46.8in)
A1.........594x841mm (23.4x33.1in)
A2.......420x594mm (16.5x23.4in)
A3........297x420mm (11.7x16.5in)

A4..........210x297mm (8.3x11.7in)
A5.............148x210mm (5.8x8.3in)
A6...............105x148mm (4.1x5.8in)
A7.................74x105mm (2.9x4.1in)

NON-OLYMPIC GAMES

Beetle herding • Bubble catching • Coin stacking
Competitive blinking • Competitive bumblebee throwing
Deep-sea eating • Endurance laughing • Stunt conkers
Heaviest-schoolbag carrying • Loudest-sneezing

—————THE FIRST FIVE GS OF ACCELERATION—————

High acceleration or deceleration subjects you to different experiences of gravity. The faster the rate of change of speed, the higher the 'g-force' and the greater the effect on your body:

1-g The effect of gravity on the surface of the Earth – you feel this all the time.

2-g The force you feel when you take off in an aeroplane. Your arms, legs, hands and feet feel heavy.

3-g The force you feel on a fast rollercoaster. You are unable to lift your head to look around and your heart has to work harder to pump blood around your body.

4-g The force you feel in a relatively minor car crash. Your head feels four times heavier, and your neck muscles struggle to cope. Your vision narrows to a small tunnel. Colours fade to white, then to black.

5-g The force felt by fighter pilots when they come out of an extremely fast turn. You may experience gravity-induced loss of consciousness, or g-loc.

—————————WHICH IS A PERFECT CIRCLE? —————

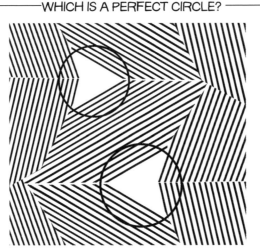

Answer: They both are

69

DO YOU SEE IN 3-D?

Hold a finger upright in front of your face, then open and close one eye at a time. Your finger appears to jump to the side. That's because each eye views from a slightly different angle. Your brain blends the images together and there you have it, a 3-D picture.

To test your 3-D vision, hold two pencils horizontally in front of you, level with your eyes. Slowly bring the tips of the two pencils together.

Easy? Now try repeating the exercise with one eye closed.

Closing one eye changes your vision to 2-D, so you can't tell which pencil is in the foreground and which is in the background.

HOW 3-D SPECS WORK

One photograph is taken, and then the camera is moved slightly and another photograph is taken from a different angle.

Both photographs are printed on the same piece of paper, one image coloured red and the other coloured blue.

3-D specs have one red and one blue lens. Looking through the red lens, the red picture seems to disappear so only the blue one can be seen, and vice versa. With each eye seeing a slightly different picture, the effect is 3-D.

YOGA POSES

Cow face • Bow • Bridge • Camel • Cat • Warrior
Downward-facing dog • One-legged king pigeon
Mountain • Half lord of the fishes • Corpse

——EXTROVERT—— OR ——INTROVERT?——

EXTROVERT	INTROVERT?
Outgoing	Reserved
Easygoing	Complicated
Thinks later	Thinks first
Emotional	Aloof
Changes the world	Understands the world
Breadth	Depth
Action	Ideas
Noise and variety	Quiet and concentration
Lots of people	One-on-one

——————ORIENTEERING MAP SYMBOLS——————

Orienteering maps are made for people who want to navigate an area on foot. Features of the landscape are shown in different colours:

Black..Rocks and man-made features

Brown..Landforms

Blue...Water features

Yellow...Easy-to-pass vegetation

Green...Difficult-to-pass vegetation

White.....................................Forest with little or no undergrowth

Purple (or red)...The orienteering course

——————MASS EXTINCTION——————

Around 249 million years ago, 90 per cent of all marine life and 70 per cent of all land animals were wiped out, including dinosaurs. This mass extinction is thought to have been the result of either an asteroid impact or massive environmental change.

─────── AN EASY METHOD ───────

You can use the following method (called a mnemonic) to remember the order of planets in our solar system: 'My Very Easy Method – Just Set Up Nine Planets'. The first letter of each of the words corresponds with the first letter of one of the planets. Mercury is the planet closest to the Sun, and Pluto is the planet furthest away from the Sun.

My...	Mercury
Very..	Venus
Easy..	Earth
Method..	Mars
Just...	Jupiter
Set..	Saturn
Up...	Uranus
Nine...	Neptune
Planets...	Pluto

─────── TEACHER, TEACHER ───────

Willy: 'Teacher, teacher, do you think it's right to punish people for things they haven't done?'

Teacher: 'Of course not.'

Willy: 'Good. I haven't done my homework.'

Teacher: 'You missed school yesterday, didn't you?'

Willy: 'Not very much, no.'

Teacher: 'Why did you eat your homework, Willy?'

Willy: 'You told me it was a piece of cake.'

Teacher: 'I wish you would pay a little attention.'

Willy: 'I can't pay anything. I didn't get my pocket money this week.'

SAILING TERMS

BROACHING
The boat suddenly tips
in the water.

DEATH ROLL
The boat rolls from side
to side until it either capsizes
or the captain takes action.

HEELING
The strength of the wind
makes the boat lean over.

HIKING
The crew lean over the
edge of the boat as it
heels to stop it tipping over.

IN IRONS
The wind blows front-on
and can push the
boat backwards.

JIBING
The boat's stern (rear) is
turned through the wind so
that the wind blows from
the other side.

TACKING
The boat's bow (front) is
turned through the wind
so that the wind blows
from the other side.

DON'T GO ZONE
The wind blows from
directly astern of (behind)
the boat, making it really
difficult to sail.

CAPSIZING
The boat overturns so that
the underside is on top.

—————————————— CONVERT IT ——————————————

inches (in)	$\xrightarrow{\times\ 2.54}$ $\xleftarrow{\times\ 0.3937}$	centimetres (cm)
feet (ft)	$\xrightarrow{\times\ 0.3048}$ $\xleftarrow{\times\ 3.2808}$	metres (m)
miles (mi)	$\xrightarrow{\times\ 1.6093}$ $\xleftarrow{\times\ 0.6214}$	kilometres (km)
square inches (sq in)	$\xrightarrow{\times\ 6.4516}$ $\xleftarrow{\times\ 0.155}$	square centimetres (cm^2)
square feet (sq ft)	$\xrightarrow{\times\ 0.0929}$ $\xleftarrow{\times\ 10.7639}$	square metres (m^2)
square miles (sq mi)	$\xrightarrow{\times\ 2.59}$ $\xleftarrow{\times\ 0.3861}$	square kilometres (km^2)
acres	$\xrightarrow{\times\ 0.4047}$ $\xleftarrow{\times\ 2.471}$	hectares
cubic inches (cu in)	$\xrightarrow{\times\ 16.3871}$ $\xleftarrow{\times\ 0.0613}$	cubic centimetres (cm^3)
pints	$\xrightarrow{\times\ 56.826}$ $\xleftarrow{\times\ 0.0176}$	centilitres (cl)
gallons (gal)	$\xrightarrow{\times\ 4.5460}$ $\xleftarrow{\times\ 0.22}$	litres (l)
ounces (oz)	$\xrightarrow{\times\ 28.3495}$ $\xleftarrow{\times\ 0.0353}$	grams (g)
pounds (lb)	$\xrightarrow{\times\ 0.454}$ $\xleftarrow{\times\ 2.2046}$	kilograms (kg)
tons (ton)	$\xrightarrow{\times\ 1016}$ $\xleftarrow{\times\ 0.001}$	kilograms (kg)

16 ounces in a pound	100 centimetres = 1 metre
12 inches in a foot	1,000 metres = 1 kilometre
2,240 pounds in a ton	1,000 grams = 1 kilogram
8 pints = 1 gallon	100 centilitres = 1 litre

—TEN WAYS A CRICKET BATSMAN CAN GET OUT—

1. Bowled
2. Caught
3. Run out
4. Stumped by the wicketkeeper
5. Hitting the ball twice
6. Touching the ball with his hand
7. Hitting his own wicket with his bat
8. LBW (standing in front of the wicket 'leg before wicket')
9. Deliberately obstructing a fielder
10. Timed out (taking longer than three minutes to walk on to the field once the previous player is out)

FICTIONAL SCHOOLS

Starfleet Academy...*Star Trek*

Springfield Elementary..*The Simpsons*

Bedrock High School...*The Flintstones*

Xavier's School For Gifted Youngsters...*X-Men*

Sunnydale High School.................................*Buffy the Vampire Slayer*

Unseen University...The Discworld novels

Midtown High School.....................Spider-Man's school in the Bronx

Imperial Academy...*Star Wars*

Pokémon Battle Judge Training Institute................................Pokémon

Hogwarts School of Witchcraft and Wizardry................The Harry Potter novels

---SILLY SUPERHEROES---

INEDIBLE MAN
Though he is only the size of a marshmallow and smells good, he tastes completely disgusting. As soon as you pop him into your mouth, the gag reflex sends him shooting across the room to fight another day.

PETER-PIPER-PICKED-A-PECK-OF-PICKLED-PEPPER MAN
'Oh no, it's Peter-Piper-Pecked-a-Pick... it's Peker-Piker-Kicked... no, it's Peper-Piper-Peped... Grrrrrrrrrr!' He is neither fast nor strong, but bad guys lose their demonic enthusiasm when they stumble on this superhero's awkward name.

SMILE MAN
Smile Man has a disarming smile. When Smile Man smiles, everybody smiles. Even bad-tempered villains can't stop grinning.

> It is impossible to fold a piece of paper of any size in half more than seven times.

---CAN YOU BUILD IT?---

────HOW TO MAKE A BALLOON SWORD────

1. Get a long, skinny balloon and
   blow it up all the way.

2. Let a little air out and tie a knot
   at the end of the balloon.

3. Make a twist in the balloon about
   10cm (4in) down from the knot
   and hold.

   This will be the handle. Don't let
   go or it will come apart.

4. Make two more twists about 8cm
   (3in) apart from each other, after
   the first twist.

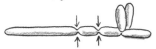

   This will form half of the cross piece of the sword.

5. Twist the first and last twist together.

6. If you now twist this with the handle you can let go of it.

7. Make two more 8cm (3in) bubbles for the second part
   of the handle, just as before.

8. Twist the last twist around the first twist to secure the
   handle in place.

9. Make any adjustments you need and straighten out
   your sword.

MOON FACTS

The Moon is 3,476km (2,160 miles) across.

The 384,400-km (238,855-mile) journey from Earth to the Moon takes a spaceship about two days. It would take an aeroplane about 26 days.

The Moon has no brightness of its own. It is lit up by the Sun.

There are dark spots on the Moon that early astronomers mistook for seas and lakes. In fact they are dry surface features, but have kept their watery names and are called things like 'The Sea of Tranquillity' and 'The Lake of Sorrow'.

SPOONERISMS

Spoonerisms are phrases where the first letters or sounds of words get mixed up through a slip of the tongue.

Pouring with rain...Roaring with pain

Block of flats...Flock of bats

Keen as mustard..Mean as custard

Lighting a fire...Fighting a liar

A half-formed wish..A half-warmed fish

I hit my funny bone.....................................I hit my bunny phone

HOOF HEARTED, ICE MELTED

Say this quickly:

'One smart man, he felt smart. Two smart men, they felt smart. Three smart men, they all felt smart.'

─────THE HISTORY OF SKATEBOARDING─────

1950   Bored surfers invent a device called a 'truck' that holds wheels to a board and allows a skater to steer the board by shifting his or her weight around.

1958   The first skateboards go on sale in a small surf shop in California, USA.

1963   The first skate contest takes place at a school in Hermosa, California.

1965   Skateboarding booms, becomes mainstream, loses its cool, then dies out.

1970   The invention of 'kick tail' boards and polyurethane wheels with bearings dramatically increase the manoeuvrability of skateboards, and the sport becomes popular again.

1978   Alan 'Ollie' Gelfand performs the first 'ollie', a skateboarding jump that almost all modern-day tricks are based on. Skaters can now jump over objects.

1981   The first edition of *Thrasher* magazine, a guide for underground skaters, is published.

1985   Vert riding (skating on ramps and other vertical structures) and streetstyle skating become popular. Professional skaters start competing for big money.

1987   'New school' skating, with an emphasis on technical tricks, becomes popular.

1990s   A focus on streetstyle and new technology shapes skateboarding into the sport it is today.

─────WAYS TO BREAK A WEREWOLF CURSE─────

Remove your animal-skin belt, in case it is enchanted

Kneel in one spot for a hundred years

Be saluted with the sign of the cross

Be addressed three times by your baptismal name

Be struck three times on the forehead with a knife, drawing
at least three drops of blood

Get someone to throw an iron object at you

─────────HOW TO MAKE A BIRD FEEDER─────────

You will need a large, open pine cone, crushed peanuts, sunflower seeds, oats, raisins, mild grated cheese, water and a length of string.

1. Mix the peanuts, sunflower seeds, oats, raisins and cheese in a bowl.

2. Add a little water to your mixture to make it sticky.

3. Push the mixture into the gaps in the pine cone.

4. Tie a piece of string around the stuffed pine cone and hang it in your garden, ideally somewhere you can see it from a window.

5. It may take a while for the birds to pluck up the courage to visit your feeder, but be patient − they will do.

─────────────DONKEY OR SEAL?─────────────

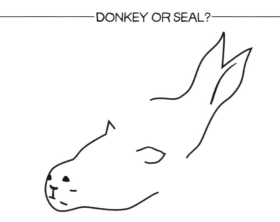

───STRANGE THINGS SOLD ON THE INTERNET───

Second-hand false teeth • Half-eaten chocolate bar
A celebrity's chewed chewing gum • Toenail clippings
An empty cardboard box • A bottle of air
A crisp packet • A person's hand in marriage

GROSS FOOD RECORDS

LARGEST CUSTARD-PIE FIGHT

The world's largest custard-pie fight was fought in Bolton, England, on 11 April 2000. A total of 3,320 custard pies were thrown by two teams of ten people in three minutes.

FASTEST KETCHUP DRINKING

On 23 September 1999, Dustin Phillips of the USA drank 91 per cent of a standard 396g (13.9oz) glass bottle of Heinz Tomato Ketchup through a drinking straw in 33 seconds.

MOST SAUSAGES SWALLOWED IN ONE MINUTE

On 13 March 2003, Cecil Walker of the USA swallowed eight whole sausages without chewing. Each sausage measured 15cm (6in) in length and 2.22cm (0.87in) in diameter.

MOST ICE CREAM EATEN IN 30 SECONDS

America's Diego Siu holds the record for eating the most ice cream in 30 seconds using a teaspoon. He consumed 264g (9.3oz) of vanilla ice cream in 30 seconds on 2 March 2003.

MOST BRUSSELS SPROUTS EATEN IN ONE MINUTE

Dave Mynard of the UK managed to eat 43 Brussels sprouts in one minute in London on 10 December 2003.

LONGEST PANCAKE MARATHON

On 24 October 1999, Mike Cuzzacrea flipped a pancake continually in a frying pan for just over three hours as he ran the 26.2-mile (40-km) New York Marathon.

————ARE YOU A BORN CRIMINAL?————

According to the theories of the 19th-century criminologist Cesare Lombroso, there are 18 key physical indicators of the born criminal:

An unusually short or tall body

Long arms

Sloping shoulders, but large chest

Pointy or stubbed fingers or toes

Wrinkles on forehead and face

Beaked or flat nose

Large, protruding ears

Strong jawline

High cheekbones

Oversized incisors

Small or weak chin

Receding hairline

Small head, but large face

Small and sloping forehead

Fleshy lips or thin upper lip

Large eye sockets, but deep-set eyes

Bumps on back of head and around ear

Bushy eyebrows, tending to meet across nose

————SMALL————	————LARGE————
Petite • Mini	Massive • Big
Little • Teeny	Gargantuan • Giant
Tiny • Miniscule	Colossal • Huge
Diminutive • Wee	Enormous • Giant
Minute • Miniature	Gigantic • Monster
Microscopic • Baby	Vast • Whopping

——————————HOW TO WHISTLE ON GRASS——————————

1. Find the biggest piece of grass you can – the taller and wider the better.
2. Press the sides of your thumbs together, with the nails facing towards you.
3. Place the piece of grass between your thumbs, so that it runs from top to bottom.
4. You will now be able to see a strip of grass in the gap between your knuckles and where your thumbs meet your hands.
5. Blow through the gap. If you don't hear a whistle at first, adjust your lips and the grass, and keep trying.

——————————SECRET SOCIETY OATH——————————

'I promise never to reveal the existence of the society to anyone else without first swearing them to the secret oath. I promise never to speak of the business of the society or to trade secrets with another society for personal gain. I promise never to reveal secret hiding places or code names. I swear this on all that is best kept secret.'

——————CITIES WITH THE MOST UNDERGROUND—————— RAILWAY LINES

New York, USA...22
Paris, France..14
London, England..12
Madrid, Spain...12
Tokyo, Japan..12
Mexico City, Mexico..11
Moscow, Russia...11
Barcelona, Spain..9
Berlin, Germany...9
Seoul, South Korea...8

——REAL LIFE—— DOUBLES

IMPERSONATOR
A person who mimics your voice and/or mannerisms.

POLITICAL DECOY
A person employed to impersonate a politician in order to draw attention away from them or to take risks on their behalf.

BODY DOUBLE
Someone who substitutes for an actor in dangerous or sexually explicit scenes.

LOOKALIKE
A living person who closely resembles another person, often a celebrity, politician or member of royalty.

——FOLKLORE—— DOUBLES

DOPPELGÄNGER
A spirit who looks exactly like you, but casts no shadow and has no reflection in a mirror or water.

SHADOWMAN
A black, human-like silhouette that lacks a mouth or eyes. It appears on the edge of your field of vision and disintegrates when noticed.

EVIL TWIN
Exists in another dimension, but occasionally enters your world through a porthole. If you catch sight of it you are in danger.

The eyes of a giant squid can be up to 40cm (15in wide)

―――――――――――― MADE INTO MUSICALS ――――――――――――

The sinking of RMS *Titanic*...*Titanic*

British Prime Minister Margaret Thatcher......*Thatcher: The Musical*

TV programme *Jerry Springer*..................*Jerry Springer: The Opera*

International cherry pit spit competition....................*Spittin' Distance*

The electric chair...*Fields of Ambrosia*

―――――――――――――― SUN FACTS ――――――――――――――

The Sun is the star at the centre of our solar system.

It is a huge ball of hydrogen and helium gas.

Earth is 150 million km (93 million miles) from the Sun.

You could fit over a million Earths into the Sun.

All the planets of our solar system, including Earth,
orbit the Sun.

The Sun is approximately 400 times wider than Earth's Moon.
The reason they appear to be about the same size is
because the Sun is 400 times further away from us.

The temperature at the Sun's core is about
16,600,000°C (28,100,000°F).

The Sun's heat and light support almost all life on Earth.

The Sun's lifetime is predicted to be around 10 billion years.
At the moment it is about 4.5 billion years old.

―――――――――――― UNCOMMON CITRUS FRUITS ――――――――――――

Ugli fruit • Buddha's hand • Dekopon
Rough lemon • Bitter orange • Kumquat
Limequat • Pomelo • Ponkan • Limetta • Natsumikan

─────────HOW TO WRITE A LIMERICK─────────

A limerick is a poem with five lines. It always has the same rhyming pattern and rhythm. The first, second and fifth lines each have eight syllables, and the final syllables of each of these lines rhyme. The middle lines both have five (or sometimes six) syllables and a different rhyme.

1. Begin by picking a boy or girl's name and write an eight-syllable line with that name at the end. For example:

   There once was a young man called Matt,

2. Make a list of words that rhyme with the last syllable in the first line — for instance, hat, cat, fat, sat, pat, rat. Now write a second eight-syllable line ending with one of your rhyming words. For example:

   Whose pet was a rat in a hat.

3. Now think of a story for your character and write two five-syllable lines with words that rhyme at the end. For example:

   The rat said, 'You know,
   The hat has to go,

4. For the final line, which will be eight syllables long, think of a resolution for your story. Go back to your list of rhyming words and be as silly as you want.

   A cat wears a hat, not a rat.'

5. Read your limerick through.

─────────ANIMALS IN ORDER OF INTELLIGENCE─────────

1. Human	8. Whale
2. Chimpanzee	9. Dolphin
3. Gorilla	10. Elephant
4. Orang-utan	11. Pig
5. Baboon	12. Dog
6. Gibbon	13. Cat
7. Monkey	14. Octopus

THE DREADED KRAKEN

Sailors beware the fabled sea monster known as the Kraken. The monster's immense, rounded back resembles an island. Desperate for dry land, sea-weary sailors have been known to drop anchor and row out to it. Before settling down for a night's rest, the fires are lit – at which the Kraken wakes up. The unfortunate sailors are drowned. Or worse.

APPLE-PIP FORTUNES

Cut an apple in half. The number of seeds you see will tell you your fortune.

One seed...Good luck

Two seeds..Marriage

Three seeds...Wealth

Four seeds...Travel

Five seeds..Health

Six seeds..Wisdom

Seven seeds...Fame

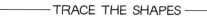

TRACE THE SHAPES

Shapes that can be traced in one continous line, without taking your pencil off the page and without tracing along any line twice:

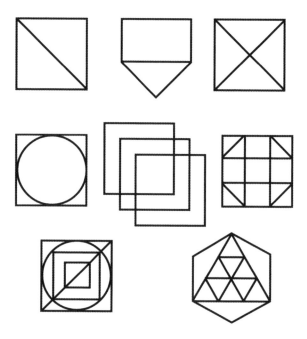

A GRUESOME EXECUTION

In 1757, the execution of Robert-François Damiens, who attempted to assassinate the French King Louis XV, began with torture using red-hot pincers. The hand with which he'd held a knife was then burnt off using sulphur. Next, molten wax, lead and boiling oil were poured into his wounds. Horses were then harnessed to his arms and legs and made to run in opposite directions so that his limbs would rip off. But his joints wouldn't tear, so the executioner had to cut through them with a knife. Even after all this agonizing torture, Damiens was rumoured not to have died, and his head and torso were later burnt at the stake.

THE POLES

The North and South Poles are the points at which the Earth's axis of rotation meets the surface of the Earth.

THE NORTH POLE

The exact North Pole, called the Geographic North Pole, is located in the Arctic Ocean. In whichever direction you travel from the Geographic North Pole, you are always heading south.

Magnetic North is the place to which all magnetic compasses point. It is not the same point as the Geographic North Pole.

The North Pole has 24 hours of daylight during the summer months and 24 hours of darkness during the winter months.

THE SOUTH POLE

The exact South Pole, called the Geographic South Pole, is located in the continent of Antarctica. In whichever direction you travel from the Geographic South Pole, you are always heading north.

The Ceremonial South Pole is an area set aside for photo opportunities a few hundred metres from the Geographic South Pole.

The ice cap at the South Pole is 3,000m (9,840ft) thick, but the ice is melting. Over 13,000 square km (8,000 square miles) of sea ice has been lost in Antarctica over the last 50 years. This is generally thought to be the consequence of global warming.

─────────────── SURF SPEAK ───────────────

Dawn patrol......................................Getting up early for a morning surf

Regular footer..............................Surfer who rides left foot forwards

Goofy footer..................................Surfer who rides right foot forwards

Kook...Hopeless surfer

Dude..Everyone and anyone

Beach breaks...Constant waves

Point breaks..Perfect waves

Gnarly...............................The sea when the waves are very choppy

Shredding...Surfing like a pro

Aerial...........................Jumping your board into the air above a wave

Wicked drop in.....................................Stealing another person's wave

Insane...Anything that's cool

Stoked...Really happy

Surfed out...In need of a rest

─────────────── TOO MUCH TV ───────────────

Goggle eyes • TV addict • Square eyes • Couch potato
Sofa sloth • Technicolour dreamer

CURSED

THE CURSE OF THE PHARAOHS

There is a belief that any person who disturbs the tomb of an ancient Egyptian pharaoh will die shortly afterwards. The curse struck the team who opened the tomb of Pharaoh Tutankhamen in 1922. Within 6 years of the tomb's discovery, 12 of the archaeologists were dead, including the expedition's patron, Lord Carnarvon, who died 47 days after entering the tomb.

THE HOPE DIAMOND

Part of the French crown jewels worn by Marie Antoinette at her execution, the diamond is thought to bring bad luck to whomever possesses it. Owners have met their deaths as a result of suicides, car crashes and cliff falls.

ANCIENT ROMAN CURSES

The ancient Romans had a formula for making an enemy suffer an injury. They wrote curses on lead tablets, known as '*tabulae defixiones*', and put them in a tomb or a sacred spring.

TECUMSEH'S CURSE

Between 1840 and 1960, all the US presidents elected in the years divisible by 20 died in office. This is said to stem from a curse issued by the Indian chief Tecumseh in 1811, when General William Henry Harrison defeated Tecumseh in battle and won the presidency. Harrison caught a cold soon after and died, having spent just one month in office. The curse was broken by Ronald Reagan, elected in 1980, who survived an assassin's bullet by less than an inch.

SCAMMER'S LANGUAGE

Con or scam...........An attempt to trick someone out of something

Grifter...The con artist

Mark or pigeon...The victim

Shill.............................A grifter's accomplice who pretends to be a member of the public as part of the scam

———————HOW TO MAKE A WATER CLOCK———————

You will need five paper cups of the same size, five drawing pins, a sturdy piece of cardboard, a glass jar as big as the cup, a narrow strip of paper, glue, a stopwatch, and a pencil.

1) Use a drawing pin to prick a hole in the bottom of each cup.

2) Pin the five cups to the cardboard, one under the other. Leave a three-finger gap between each cup.

3) Stick the strip of paper vertically to the glass jar and put the jar under the bottom cup.

4) Fill the top cup with water and check that it drips through each cup into the jar at the bottom.

5) OK? Then do it again, using the same water, but this time start your stopwatch at the moment you start pouring.

6) At intervals of 5 minutes, mark the water level on the paper on your jar.

7) When all the water has dripped into the jar, you can use this 'clock' to keep track of time.

———REAL PARTS——— OF A SWISS ARMY KNIFE	———PARTS OF A——— SWISS ARMY KNIFE NOT YET INVENTED
Large blade	Skeleton key
Small blade	Grappling hook
Corkscrew	Pea-shooter
Can opener	Industrial laser
Small screwdriver	Bugging device
Bottle opener	Miniature fishing reel
Pliers	Universal remote control
Tweezers	Digital voice recorder
Torch	Invisible ink pen
Scissors	Telescope

SYMMETRICAL WORDS

If you were to draw a horizontal line through the middle of the following words, the top of the word would be a miror image of the bottom:

COOKBOOK	BIKED
EXCEEDED	DICED
HOODED	CHOKE
DEED	CHOICE
BEDECKED	HIKED
CHEEK	BOBBED

THE OLDEST EVER

Marine clam	200 years old
Human	122 years old
Elephant	78 years old
Giant tortoise	75 years old
Horse	62 years old
Dog	29 years old
Mouse	4 years old

It takes just $\frac{1}{50}$ of a second for the guillotine blade to sever the head from the neck, though it has been suggested that it may take up to 7 seconds for the brain to lose consciousness after the head is severed.

IS THIS ART?

Some important modern artworks have included:

A urinal
A pile of bricks
An unmade bed
A rubbish bin
A black canvas
A sheep cut in half
A wrapped-up dog kennel
An empty room with a light
bulb that repeatedly goes
on and off

HOW TO MAKE A COMPASS

You will need a clear glass bowl filled with water, a 0.5-cm (0.2-in) slice from the end of a cork, a magnet and a needle.

1. Float the cork in the bowl of water.

2. Magnetize the needle by rubbing it over the magnet in the same direction about fifty times.

3. Lay the needle on the cork.

The needle will slowly turn to line up with the Earth's North and South Magnetic Poles.

LOUDEST EVER HUMAN NOISES

Knuckle crack...........108 decibels, Bob Hatch, USA, 17 May 2000

Burp.....................................118.1 decibels, Paul Hunn, UK, 5 April 2000

Scream....................129 decibels, Jill Drake, UK, 22 October 2000

———— HOW TO CHART YOUR FAMILY TREE ————

1. Write your name at the bottom of a large piece of paper.

2. If you have any brothers or sisters, write their names alongside yours, oldest on the left, youngest on the right.

3. Draw a vertical line out of the top of each of the names. Finish each line at the same point, then join the top of the lines together with a horizontal line.

4. Draw a vertical line upwards from the centre of the horizontal line.

5. Starting at the top of the vertical line, draw a short horizontal line to either side.

6. Write your father's name on the left of the line and your mother's name on the right. Your family tree should now look something like this:

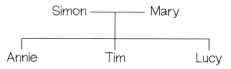

7. Write the names of your father's brothers and sisters to the left of his name, and your mother's brothers and sisters to the right of her name, in age order from left to right.

8. Connect the names of the brothers and sisters in your father's family, and draw a vertical line to the names of their parents (your grandparents) in the same way you connected the names of the children in your family to your parents. Now do the same for your mother's side of the family.

9. Write the names of your grandparents' brothers and sisters next to your grandparents' names, and connect them to the names of their parents (your great-grandparents).

10. Continue this pattern to trace your family tree back as far as you can – ask your relatives to help you find out all the names. You may also wish to add everyone's date of birth.

HOMEMADE INSTRUMENTS

DRUMS
Stretch different materials (such as carrier bags or balloons) tightly over pots of different sizes using elastic bands, and strike with a salad spoon.

MARACAS
Fill a plastic water bottle, film canister, or tea caddy with rice, pebbles, coffee beans, or sand. Vitamin-tablet pots are ready-made maracas.

CYMBALS
Bang two saucepan lids together.

XYLOPHONES
Fill drinking glasses or glass bottles with varying amounts of water and line them up from most to least full. Tap each glass with a pencil to produce different notes.

The ancient Greek mathematician Hero invented the vending machine in Alexandria. The coin dropped on to a lever which opened a valve and out flowed a small amount of holy water.

———— TIPS FOR AVOIDING BEE STINGS ————

1. Never try to swat a honeybee. Bees are generally passive unless annoyed or threatened, and usually only sting in self-defence.

2. Smell horrible. Bees like flowers that smell nice. You stink, they fly away.

3. Wear camouflage. Bees have poor eyesight and won't be able to spot you wearing light colours in the day and dark colours at night.

4. Never mow the lawn. The low buzzing of motorized garden tools can agitate swarms, hives or colonies.

5. Keep your shoes on. Particularly avoid walking barefoot over lawns that contain blooming clover, which bees love.

6. If a bee head-butts you, move quickly in the opposite direction. Sentry bees patrolling the edges of the hive's territory do this to warn off invaders.

7. Stay indoors until sunset. Bees generally sleep after dark.

———— THE SPEED YOU MAKE THE AIR MOVE ————

Inhaling	6kph (4mph)
Sniffing	30kph (20mph)
Coughing	100kph (60mph)
Sneezing	160kph (100mph)

———— RETIRED HURRICANE NAMES ————

All hurricanes are given a name from a long list. If an unusually destructive hurricane hits, its name is retired and never used again. Among those retired are:

Allison • Floyd • Georges • Keith
Iris • Lenny • Michelle

──────── SPONTANEOUS HUMAN COMBUSTION ────────

Throughout history, there have been many documented cases of people going up in flames for no apparent reason. The following evidence makes it look as though the flames that devoured the victims came from inside their own bodies:

Despite its severity, the fire is confined to the body. Clothing is barely singed, and flammable objects nearby remain untouched.

Portions of the body, such as an arm or a foot, remain unburned.

The torso usually suffers severe burning and in some cases is reduced to ash.

A greasy soot deposit covers the ceiling and walls.

Suggested but unconvincing theories for spontaneous human combustion include:

Static electricity build-up

Flammable body fat

The short-circuiting of the body's electrical fields

An explosive combination of digestive chemicals

High levels of alcohol in the body

──────────── THE LONGEST-EVER HAIRS ────────────

Longest eyebrow.............................7.81cm (3.07in), Franklin Ames, USA

Longest leg hair..............................12.4cm (4.8in), Tim Stinton, Australia

Longest ear hair.........................13.2cm (5.2in), Radhakant Bajpai, India

Longest female beard....................27.9cm (11in), Vivian Wheeler, USA

---MATCHSTICK PUZZLE---

Take away nine matches to form only four squares.
All squares (large and small) are counted and each
match must be part of a square.

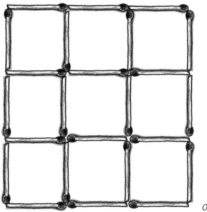

Answer on page 120

--- HOW TO PLAY 'CUPS'---

1. This is a game to be played in a swimming pool, lake
   or the sea. Two players stand back-to-back in waist-
   deep water.

2. Choose one player to be the cupper and one person to
   be the guesser.

3. At the count of three, both players must duck underwater.
   The cupper then swims one stroke either to the left or to
   the right. At the same time, the guesser swims one stroke
   in the direction that they think the cupper will have swum.

4. If, when both players resurface, they are in the same place,
   the guesser has guessed correctly and takes the point. If
   they are two strokes apart, the cupper has outsmarted
   the guesser and the cupper takes the point.

5. After three games, the player with the most wins takes
   the role of the cupper.

———————— THE OFFSIDE RULE IN SOCCER ————————

The offside rule is said to be soccer's most complicated rule. Understanding the rule traditionally distinguishes real soccer fans from everyone else.

An attacking player is in an offside position if he is nearer his opponents' goal line than both the ball and the last defender (not including the goalie).

However, the player is only penalized for being in an offside position if his team gain an advantage from it at the moment the ball is played by one of his teammates.

When defenders deliberately move forwards to try to put an attacker offside, it is known as the 'offside trap'.

There is no offence if the offside player receives the ball directly from a goal kick, throw-in or corner kick.

If you get stuck in the middle of your spaceship in zero gravity and are unable to reach the floor, ceiling or walls, do not despair. Instead, take off a shoe and throw it across the cabin. You and your shoe will act as a pair of equal and opposite forces, propelling you backwards. The harder you throw your shoe, the faster you will be pushed away from it.

———————— EMBARRASSED AT SCHOOL ————————

Your mum kisses you goodbye at the school gate.

Your sister follows you, calling you by your family nickname.

You get chosen last when picking teams for P.E.

Your parents make friends with the parents of the school geek, and they arrange for you all to go on holiday together.

There's a stink in the toilets. Everyone's talking about it, and you're responsible.

FAMOUS LAST WORDS

THE SCIENTIST
The 19th-century British surgeon Joseph Henry Green checked his own pulse, announced 'Stopped,' and then died.

THE POET
The German poet Heinrich Heine never got to give his last message to the world, his final words being 'Write... write... pencil... paper.'

THE PLAYWRIGHT
The Norwegian dramatist Henrik Ibsen heard his nurse tell a visitor that he was feeling better. 'On the contrary,' Ibsen said, and died.

THE ACTOR
Hollywood swashbuckler Douglas Fairbanks declared 'I've never felt better,' and promptly died.

THE PHILOSOPHER
The German political philosopher Karl Marx was asked by his maid if he had any last words. He replied, 'Go on, get out! Last words are for fools who haven't said enough!'

THE WIT
The last words of Oscar Wilde are believed to be: 'Either this wallpaper goes, or I do.'

You can't stop yourself vomiting by keeping your mouth shut. The sick will just come out of your nose instead.

—HOW NOT TO GET EATEN BY A POLAR BEAR—

1. Keep a clean camp. Bears can sniff food, and rubbish smells from a long way away.

2. Stay away from mammal carcasses.

3. Never pet a polar bear cub.

IF A POLAR BEAR APPROACHES...

1. Stand your ground.

2. Make yourself look bigger by holding a jacket over your head.

3. Shout at the bear.

4. If all else fails, throw the bear your sandwiches and run.

—FAKE HARRY POTTER BOOKS IN CHINA—

Harry Potter and the Porcelain Doll
Harry Potter and the Leopard-Walk-Up-To-Dragon
Harry Potter and the Golden Turtle
Harry Potter and the Crystal Vase

What do astronauts drink?

Gravi-tea

CLOTHING SIZES AROUND THE WORLD

WOMEN'S CLOTHES

American	8	10	12	14	16	18
British	10	12	14	16	18	20
Continental	38	40	42	44	46	48

MEN'S CLOTHES

American	36	38	40	42	44	46
British	36	38	40	42	44	46
Continental	46	48	50	52	54	56

CHILDREN'S CLOTHES

American	4	6	8	10	12	14
British						
Height (in)	36	38	40	42	44	46
Age	4–5	6–8	9–10	11	12	13
Continental						
Height (cm)	125	135	150	155	160	165
Age	7	9	12	13	14	15

Army ants of South America don't have nests. They live on the move, foraging as they go. Anything in their path, including animals, is likely to be eaten alive.

A LIGHT BULB PROBLEM

You are in a room with three light switches labelled 1, 2, 3. One of the light switches controls a bulb you can't see that is in the next room. All three switches are off and the light bulb is off. You can flick any of the switches as many times as you want, for as long as you want. You can then go into the next room once to check the bulb. How will you find out which switch is connected to the bulb?

Turn switch 1 on for 10 minutes, then turn it off. Turn switch 2 on then immediately go to check the bulb. If it is off and hot it is switch 1. If it is on it is switch 2. If it is off and cold it is switch 3.

——CHRISTMAS DINNERS AROUND THE WORLD——

Turkey...Salted dry cod with boiled potatoes

Transylvania..Stuffed cabbage

Russia..Meat dumplings

Sweden.............Baked ham, pickled herring, lutfish and rice pudding

Poland...Beetroot soup, prune dumplings, carp

Britain...Roasted goose

Germany...Carp or goose

USA..Roasted turkey

————————ONE YEAR IN SPACE————————

A year is the amount of time it takes
for a planet to go around the Sun.

PLANET	DISTANCE FROM SUN (million miles)	LENGTH OF YEAR (in Earth days)
Mercury	36	88
Venus	67	225
Earth	93	365
Mars	142	687
Jupiter	484	4,333
Saturn	887	10,750
Uranus	1,784	30,707
Neptune	2,796	60,202
Pluto	3,666	90,803

The one-syllable word 'are' can be
changed into a three-syllable word by
adding the single letter 'a' to the end of it.

REALLY LONG WALKS

THE MEDIEVAL PILGRIMAGE
Medieval pilgrims walked 1,600km (1,000 miles) from France to reach the holy shrine in Santiago de Compostela in Spain.

THE APPALACHIAN TRAIL
This 3,487-km (2,167-mile) trail through the Appalachian Mountains of America is the longest hiking trail in the world.

THE SILK ROAD
In 100BC Chinese silk merchants travelled 6,000km (3,700 miles) along the Silk Road from China to Imperial Rome.

THE GREAT WALL OF CHINA
Also known as 'the longest graveyard on Earth', this ancient fortification stretches 2,400km (1,500 miles) through scorching deserts, mountains and dangerous forests.

HOW WATERY?

A tomato...95 per cent

A potato...80 per cent

A human...75 per cent

A loaf of bread..35 per cent

─────THE FORMING OF THE CONTINENTS─────

By looking at the structure of the Earth, it is possible
to form theories about how the continents we
have today came into being.

YEARS AGO	CONTINENTS
3 billion	There was one continent called Ur
	which split into
2.5 billion	Ur and Arctica
	which split into
2 billion	Ur, Arctica, Baltica and Atlantica
	then Arctica and Baltica joined to form Nena, so the continents were
1.5 billion	Nena, Ur and Atlantica
	then Nena, Ur and Atlantica joined to form
1 billion	Rodinia
	which split into
700 million	Nena, Atlantica and Ur
	which joined again to form
300 million	Pangaea
	which eventually split into
200 million	Africa, Antarctica, Australia, Europe, Asia, and North and South America

─────GREETINGS IN DIFFERENT COUNTRIES─────

Japan..............Bow from the waist, palms on thighs, heels together

France..A kiss on both cheeks

New Zealand Maoris..A touching of noses

Britain...A handshake

India..With palms pressed together as though
praying, a bend or nod

MAJOR RISKS OF SPACE TRAVEL

Becoming separated from the ship during a space-walk
Blacking out during take-off
Crash-landing on an airless planet
Being hit by a meteor
Being exposed to radiation
Burning up on re-entering the Earth's atmosphere

EINSTEIN'S PUZZLE

Three dragons, Dudley, Delilah and Dave, live in three separate holes, numbered 1, 2, 3 from left to right. They each have a favourite rock band (The Scaly Singers, The Winged Wonders and The Fire Breathers) and a favourite ice cream flavour (vanilla, strawberry and chocolate). Based on the following information, which dragon loves chocolate ice cream and which dragon listens to The Scaly Singers?

Dudley loves vanilla ice cream

Delilah's favourite rock band is The Fire Breathers.

The dragon that lives in the left hole is a fan of
The Winged Wonders.

Dudley and Delilah have one hole separating them.

The Scaly Singers fan does not live on the left of
the strawberry ice cream lover.

ANSWER - Delilah loves chocolate ice cream. Dave listens to The Scaly Singers

---HAND SHADOWS---

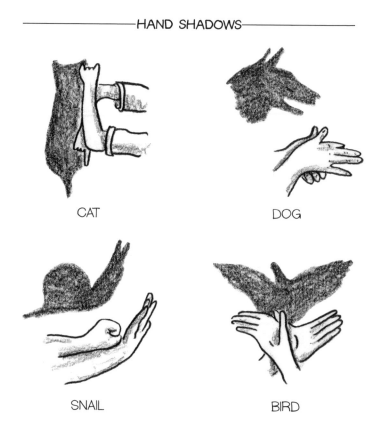

CAT

DOG

SNAIL

BIRD

---GALILEO'S SHIP---

You are in a cabin below the deck of a ship. You have with
you: two goldfish in a bowl, a ball and a stick of incense.
When the boat is at anchor, the goldfish swim with equal effort
in all directions, the ball falls straight down from your hands to
the floor, and the incense smoke drifts directly upwards
into the air. When the boat is moving in a straight line and
at an even pace, will these effects change?

*Answer: No. Everything contained in the ship, including the air, is moving at
the same rate.*

---HIGH DIVING---

BACKWARD
The diver takes off with his
or her back to the water.

PIKE
The body is folded in half,
bent at the waist but
not at the knees.

LAYOUT
The body is
completely straight.

TUCK
The body is curled into
a ball, with the knees
brought up to the chin and
the heels tucked against
the back of the legs.

WATER ENTRANCE
The diver must be straight,
powerful and make a
minimal splash.

The world's highest ever dive, a double-back somersault from 54m (177ft), was performed by the Swiss diver Oliver Favre in Villers-le-Lac, France, in 1987.

In 1998, the Swiss diver Frederic Weill performed a dive from a helicopter into Lake Verbano in Italy. The 26m (86ft) dive included an armstand take-off and double somersault pike.

The highest ever shallow dive was performed by Danny Higginbottom from Louisiana, USA, on 8 September 2004. He dived from a height of 8.95m (29ft 4in) into 30cm (1ft) of water.

Camels' humps do not contain water as is commonly believed, but instead store fatty tissue that can be converted to water. The fat supply is enough for them to survive without a drink for about two weeks, and without food for up to a month.

EGYPTIAN HIEROGLYPHS

Ancient Egyptians wrote using hieroglyphics – a script made up of pictures. There are few clues as to how Egyptians pronounced their words, but here are some hieroglyphs that roughly translate to the letters of our alphabet (there is no equivalent for 'x').

a
as in 'ant'

b
as in 'bat'

c
as in 'loch'

d
as in 'dad'

e
as in 'eat'

f
as in 'fog'

g
as in 'got'

h
as in 'hat'

i
as in 'pin'

j
as in 'jump'

k
as in 'kite'

l
as in 'lot'

m
as in 'mum'

n
as in 'not'

o
as in 'who'

p
as in 'pin'

q
as in 'quit'

r
as in 'run'

s
as in 'sit'

t
as in 'top'

u
as in 'glue'

v
as in 'van'

w
as in 'wig'

y
as in 'baby'

z
as in 'zoo'

WHAT KIND OF -PHILE ARE YOU?

'-phile' is the opposite of '-phobe'
and means 'loving'.

Turophile..Cheese

Hippophile...Horses

Ophiophile...Snakes

Nyctophile..Darkness

Hoplophile...Weaponry

Xylophile..Wood

Logophile..Words

Technophile...Technology

Claustrophile...Enclosed spaces

Thalassophile..Seas

Francophile...France

Bibliophile...Books

TYPES OF FIREWORK

Star shells • Mini mines • Mini bombettes • Salutes • Jacks
Cones • Helicopters • Planes • UFOs • Snakes • Racers
Bottle rockets • Catherine wheels • Bangers

WHAT'S THE DIFFERENCE?

INDIAN AND AFRICAN ELEPHANTS
The African elephant is larger than the Indian elephant and has larger ears. The African elephant has two lips on its trunk, while the Indian elephant has only one.

STALAGMITES AND STALACTITES
These icicle-shaped pillars form over thousands of years where water drips through the roof of a limestone cave, leaving mineral deposits behind. Stalagmites grow up from the ground while stalactites grow down from the roof of the cave.

INTERNET AND THE WORLD WIDE WEB
The Internet is a massive network in which any computer can communicate with any other computer as long as they are both connected to the Internet. The World Wide Web is just one way of accessing information on the Internet. It uses a computer-programming language called HTTP. This is just one of the many languages used over the Internet.

COCA-COLA AND PEPSI-COLA
Coca-Cola was invented in 1886, followed by Pepsi in 1898. It is assumed that Coca-Cola was named after the coca leaves and kola nuts used to make it. Pepsi was named after the beneficial effects it was believed to have on a kind of bellyache called dyspepsia.

MONOPOLY RECORDS

Longest anti-gravitational game (played on the ceiling)....36 hours

Longest game played in a bath..99 hours

Longest game played in a lift...16 days

Longest game played underwater..45 days

Longest game ever played..70 days

─── A KNOT TRICK ───

Challenge your friends to tie a knot in a piece of string without letting go of the ends. Then, when they've got themselves into a tangle, you can show them how it's done.

Lay the piece of string in front of you and cross your arms so that one hand is over the other arm and one hand is under.

Keeping your arms folded, pick up each end of the string.

Keeping hold of the two ends, uncross your arms.

Ta-da! The string is tied in a knot.

Ostriches can run at 72kph (45mph) for nearly 20 minutes at a time.

HOW TO EAT IN A POSH RESTAURANT

DO	DON'T
Put your napkin on your knee straight away.	Lean your elbows on the table.
Start with the outer cutlery and work your way in with each course.	Eat French fries with your fingers.
Finish your mouthful before sipping water.	Chew ice at the table.
Say 'Excuse me' if you need to leave the table.	Eat with your mouth open.
	Yell at the waiter.
	Say 'Urghhhh!' if you don't like something.

THE LARGEST COUNTRIES

Russia.............................17,075,200 square km (6,592,735 square miles)

Canada..........................9,976,140 square km (3,851,788 square miles)

China..............................9,596,960 square km (3,705,386 square miles)

USA.................................9,372,610 square km (3,618,764 square miles)

Brazil..............................8,511,965 square km (3,286,470 square miles)

Australia........................7,686,850 square km (2,967,893 square miles)

WORLD STANDARDS

METRE

A metre was originally a French standard of measurement. It was said to be one ten-millionth part of the distance from the North Pole to the equator, when measured on a straight line running along the surface of the Earth through Paris. Today, a metre is the distance travelled by light in a vacuum during 1/299,792,458 of a second.

FATHOM

Sailors used to measure the depth of water using a long, weighted rope called a sounding line. A fathom was the length of rope that a man could hold between his extended arms as he hauled it out of the sea. One fathom is 1.8m (6ft) long. In old English the word 'fathom' means 'outstretched arm'.

MILE

Roman soldiers kept track of the distances they marched by counting their paces. One pace was a double step. One mile was a thousand paces – in Latin, *mille passas*.

> What is a robot's favourite part of the school day?
>
> Assembly

LIZARD NAMES

Alectrosaurus	Unmarried lizard
Deinodon	Terrible tooth
Gasosaurus	Gas lizard
Nanosaurus	Dwarf lizard
Quaesitosaurus	Abnormal lizard
Saichania	Beautiful one
Ultrasaurus	Ultra giant lizard
Xenotarsosaurus	Strange-ankle lizard

A WITCH'S SPELL

Double, double toil and trouble;
Fire burn, and cauldron bubble.

...

Fillet of a fenny snake,
In the cauldron boil and bake;
Eye of newt and toe of frog,
Wool of bat and tongue of dog,
Adder's fork and blind-worm's sting;
Lizard's leg and howlet's wing,
For a charm of powerful trouble,
Like a hell-broth boil and bubble.

...

Double, double toil and trouble;
Fire burn, and cauldron bubble.

...

Cool it with a baboon's blood,
Then the charm is firm and good.

A camel-hair brush is made of squirrel fur.

TEXTOGRAMS

Textograms are words formed from the same number
sequence on a telephone keypad. They are often
mixed up when texting.

269	boy, box, cow
4663	home, good, gone, hood, hoof
328	fat, eat
7664	snog, song
2253	bake, cake, bald, calf
5693	love, loud

RIVERS FROM SOURCE TO SEA

THE NILE
Source: Lake Victoria, east-central Africa
Sea: Mediterranean Sea
Journey: 6,695km (4,160 miles)

THE GANGES
Source: Himalayan Mountains
Sea: Indian Ocean
Journey: 2,510km (1,560 miles)

THE AMAZON
Source: Andes Mountains, Peru
Sea: Atlantic Ocean
Journey: 6,275km (3,899 miles)

THE RHINE
Source: Swiss Alps
Sea: North Sea
Journey: 1,320km (820 miles)

THE MISSISSIPPI
Source: Lake Itasca, Minnesota
Sea: Gulf of Mexico
Journey: 3,705 km (2,302 miles)

THE THAMES
Source: Cotswolds, England
Sea: North Sea
Journey: 340km (210 miles)

THE YANGTZE
Source: Kunlun Mountains, western China
Sea: Pacific Ocean
Journey: 6,300km (3,915 miles)

THE DANUBE
Source: Black Forest, Germany
Sea: Black Sea
Journey: 2,850km (1,771 miles)

WHICH MIDDLE CIRCLE IS BIGGEST?

Answer: they are both the same size.

FUN RACES

INDIVIDUAL EVENTS

EGG-AND-SPOON RACE: The competitor must complete the race without dropping a hard-boiled egg balanced on a spoon.

PANCAKE RACE: At certain points in the race the competitor must successfully flip a pancake in the frying pan he or she is running with.

SACK RACE: The competitor places both legs inside a sack and hops or shuffles to the finishing line.

DOUBLE ACTS

THREE-LEGGED RACE: The competitors tie their inside legs together and run in tandem.

PIGGYBACK RACE: The lighter competitor climbs on the heavier or stronger competitor's back and is carried to the finishing line.

WHEELBARROW RACE: One competitor runs on his or her hands while the other follows behind holding their teammate's legs in the air.

LIFE ON MARS

The surface of Mars is thought to be mainly composed of a black volcanic rock called basalt, which is also found on Earth.

In December 1984, a Martian meteorite was found in Antarctica. It is thought to have contained fossils of microscopic bacteria that lived on Mars millions of years ago.

In 2004, the orbiting probe *Mars Express* found methane in the Martian atmosphere. On Earth, methane is emitted by primitive life forms.

TV FIRSTS

1926   The Scottish engineer John Logie Baird gives the first public demonstration of a working television set in London.

1951   The world's first colour programme is broadcast in the USA. It is a musical variety show.

1955   The first wireless remote control is launched. It is called the 'Zenith Flash-matic'.

1964   The plasma display monitor is invented.

1967   The first video game for a television set is launched. It is called *Chase*.

1969   A camera in the lunar module provides live television coverage as Neil Armstrong becomes the first man to walk on the Moon. Approximately 600 million people tune in.

1975   Sony launch the 'Betamax' home recording system. The system allows consumers to record and play back television programmes.

1975   The band Queen produce the first successful pop video. It is to their song *Bohemian Rhapsody*.

1976   The Japanese company JVC launch the 'VHS' home recording system to rival Sony's 'Betamax'.

1996   The first DVD players and discs are sold in Japan.

SPY CODE

Ears Only..........................Documents too secret to commit to writing

Eyes Only................Documents that may be read but not discussed

Wet Job...An operation in which blood is shed

Dead Drop..........................Secret locations where messages are left

Black Operations..........Secret operations that no one owns up to

Mole...An agent sent to gather intelligence by working or living among the enemy

———WHO IS THE PATRON SAINT OF WHAT?———

Maria Goretti..Girls

John Bosco...Boys

Roch..Dogs

Francis of Assisi..Animals

Gabriel of Our Lady of Sorrows...Students

Amand...Scouts

Joseph of Cupertino..Astronauts

Fiacre..Taxi drivers

Isidore of Seville..Computer programmers

Clare of Assisi..Television

Barbara..Fireworks

Francis de Sales..Teachers

———THE PERPETUALLY ASCENDING STAIRCASE———

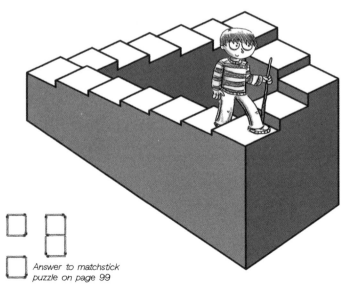

*Answer to matchstick
puzzle on page 99*

ARE YOU TELEPATHIC?

Sit back-to-back with a friend and decide who will be the sender and who will be the receiver.

The sender calls 'Go!' and draws a simple diagram, for example a square, circle or triangle.

The sender concentrates hard on 'sending' the image to the receiver.

The receiver draws whatever comes into his or her mind.

Compare the drawings, looking for similarities. For example, a triangle may be telepathically received as the sail of a boat.

In May 2005, a US hot-dog company made a 22.9m (75ft)- long hot dog, some 120 times longer than your average sausage.

MEDIEVAL WEAPONS

Knight's sword..............................Single-handed, cross-shaped sword

Claymore..................Large, two-handed sword used in clan warfare

Sabre..Curved sword with large hand guard

Bludgeon.....................One- or two-handed club for whacking things

War hammer........Hammer with one blunt end and one spiked end

Pike.............Long, spear-like weapon used against cavalry assaults

Arbalest..................................Large, tremendously powerful crossbow

Flail..................Spiked metal ball(s) attached to a handle by a chain

Morning star.............Pole with a spherical head with a large spike on its end, and smaller spikes around its circumference

——THE GEORGE WASHINGTON CONUNDRUM——

When he was a boy, the person who became the first President of the USA allegedly cut down his father's cherry tree. The axe he used is on display in a museum, although, having had both its handle and head replaced several times, no part of the original axe remains.

————MAN-MADE OBJECTS LEFT ON MARS————

Mars 2..	USSR, 1971
Viking 1..	USA, 1976
Mars Pathfinder..	USA, 1997
Mars Polar Lander..	USA, 1999
Beagle 2..	Europe, 2003
MER B..	USA, 2004

> Spun sugar is called candy floss in the UK, *barbe à papa* in France, *Zuckerwatte* in Germany, fairy floss in Australia and cotton candy in the United States.

———————PRO-WRESTLING MOVES———————

Armbreaker • Atomic Drop
Powerslam • Twist of Fate
Brainbuster • Body Slam
Death Valley Driver
Russian Legsweep
Frankensteiner
Huracarrana
Irish Whip
Facebreaker
Electric Chair Bomb

WITCHES

During the 1600s many women in Europe and America were accused of being witches. One of the most common ways of telling if a woman was a witch was to bind her right thumb to her left toe and throw her in a river. If she floated she would be found guilty and executed. If she sank she would be found innocent, but of course she died anyway. A woman could be found guilty of witchcraft if:

She was afraid during the trial

She didn't cry during the trial

She had an unusual mark on her body

She could not feel the prick of a pin

A member of her family was thought to be a witch

She looked 'witchy'

ANIMAL SIXTH SENSE

AMPULLAE OF LORENZI

This special organ enables sharks to detect weak electrical stimuli from the muscle movements of prey that are hidden or distant.

BUTTERFLY TARSI

The 'tarsi', or feet, of the American painted lady have special sensors that allow the butterfly to detect sweet food.

LATERAL LINE

Fish use this sense organ to detect changes in water pressure and feel the movement of other animals in the water nearby.

JACOBSEN'S ORGAN

Snakes use this organ to 'taste' prey. Their forked tongues collect chemicals from the air and bring them into the mouth, where the organ is located.

A hair transplant involves the removal of a patch of hairy scalp from the head. Hundreds of individual hairs or hair clusters are then taken from the patch under a magnifying glass and sewn back into the scalp to cover the bald area.

AN ETHICAL PROBLEM

A runaway train is hurtling towards five people tied to a railway track. You can save them by pulling a lever that steers the train down a branch line. Unfortunately, there is a single person tied to the branch line. Do you pull the lever?

INTERNATIONAL DIALLING CODES

Antarctica...+672

Australia..+61

France..+33

Germany...+49

Greece...+30

Italy...+39

Mongolia...+976

Netherlands..+31

Poland..+48

Spain..+34

Switzerland..+41

UK...+44

USA..+1

HOW TO INSULT SOMEONE AND GET AWAY WITH IT

With this list of posh put-downs you'll never be short of something to say to unsuspecting friends and family, and you'll never get into trouble. Even your teacher will be flabbergasted.

asinine (ass-in-ine) — very stupid:
'That was an asinine thing to do.'

blatherskite (blather-skite) — a person who talks nonsense:
'What a blatherskite you are!'

cacophony (ka-koff-funny) — unpleasantly loud noise:
'What a cacophony my sister is making with her singing!'

discombobulate (dis-kom-bob-u-late) — confuse:
'He was totally discombobulated by what I said.'

lollapalooza (lolla-palooza) — a particularly attractive or impressive thing or person:
'He's no lollapalooza in his school uniform.'

noisome (noy-some) — stinking, extremely unpleasant:
'My brother's bedroom is very noisome.'

tawdry (tordry) — something flashy, but of rubbish quality:
'Auntie, what fabulously tawdry jewellery you are wearing!'

technophobe (tekno-fobe) — someone who dislikes or fears new technology:
'My dad can't even answer his mobile phone. He's a real technophobe.'

temerity (tim-erity) — extreme boldness and cheek:
'What temerity to insult people like this!'

The goliath bird-eating spider, a type of tarantula living in the South American jungle, is recorded as the world's biggest spider. It has a leg span of around 28cm (11in).

GOODBYE

So long

Farewell

Cheerio

Ta ta

See you later, alligator

In a while, crocodile

CHILDREN'S MISCELLANY

THE COLLECTION

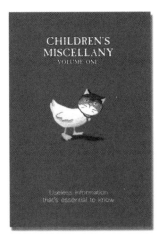

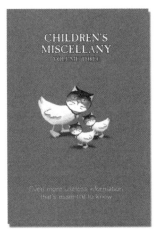

Three volumes of
useless information
that's essential
to know.

VOLUME ONE
ISBN-10: 1-904613-65-9
ISBN-13: 978-1-904613-65-7

VOLUME TWO
ISBN-10: 1-905158-16-5
ISBN-13: 978-1-905158-16-4

VOLUME THREE
ISBN-10: 1-905158-42-4
ISBN-13: 978-1-905158-42-3